THE HERMIT FATHERS

By: FR. SAMAAN EL SOURIANY

Translated By
Lisa Agaiby & Mary Girgis

St Shenouda Coptic Orthodox Monastery
Putty, NSW, Australia

Title: The Hermit Fathers
Author: Fr Samaan El Souriany
Translated by: Mary Girgis
Edited by: Lisa Agaiby

First Edition 1993

Published by: Coptic Orthodox Publication and Translation
                 P.O. Box B63
                 Bexley N.S.W. 2207
                 Sydney, Australia
ISBN: 0 908000 17 0

Second Edition 2008

Published by: St Shenouda Coptic Orthodox Monastery
                 8419 Putty Rd
                 Putty, N.S.W. 2330
                 Sydney, Australia
ISBN: 978-0-9805171-0-1

Cover Design: Daniel Fanous
Cover Illustration: An icon of five well known Hermit fathers
Back Row (L-R):   Abba Misail, Abba Karas, Abba Galion
Front Row (L-R): Abba Paula, Abba Thomas, Abba Noufer

The second edition was published with the kind permission of
Mary Girgis and Lisa Agaiby

Printed in Australia

ii

H.H. Pope Shenouda III,
117th Pope of Alexandria
and the Sea of St. Mark

When St. Macarius the great returned to his monastery, and after seeing two of the anchorites in the wilderness, said to his disciples:

"I am not a monk, but I have seen monks!"

The anchoritic life represents a life of a person who has completely died to the world to live in God and God in him. They left all comforts of the world so that God will become their only comfort. Who can write the life of these anchorites? Or who knows what their daily routine. How did they start their life of anchoritism? Who saw them and wrote about them? But as for their spirituality and life with God, they are the holy of holies. When we talk about the lives of the anchorites we are only touching the outer surface of their life.

H.H. Pope Shenouda III

TABLE OF CONTENTS

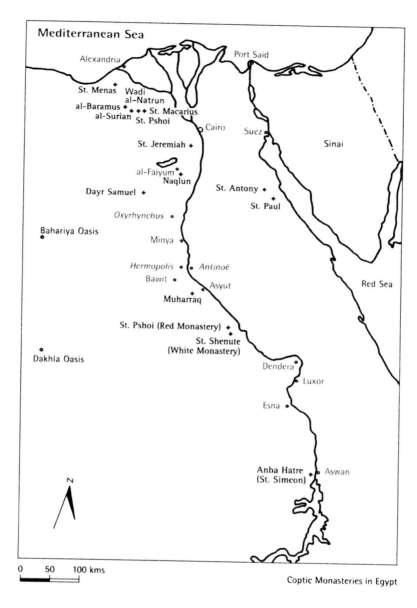

Mediterranean Sea

Alexandria
Port Said

St. Menas
Wadi
al-Natrun
al-Baramus
al-Surian
St. Macarius
St. Pshoi
Cairo
Suez
Sinai

St. Jeremiah

al-Faiyum
Naqlun
St. Antony
St. Paul

Dayr Samuel

Oxyrhynchus

Bahariya Oasis

Minya

Hermopolis
Antinoë
Bawit
Asyut
Red Sea

Muharraq

St. Pshoi (Red Monastery)
St. Shenute
(White Monastery)

Dakhla Oasis

Dendera
Luxor

Esna

N

Anba Hatre
(St. Simeon)
Aswan

0   50   100 kms

Coptic Monasteries in Egypt

(Gawdat Gabra, Coptic Monasteries. Egypt's Monastic Art
and Architecture, Cairo 2002, p. XV.)

- 1 -

FOREWORD

The Historical Background - The great centre for monasticism was Egypt. By AD 400 Egypt was a land of hermits and monks. There were three main types of monasticism there, corresponding very roughly to three geographical locations.

Lower Egypt - The hermit life. The prototype of the hermit life was St. Anthony the Great, a Copt and a layman. He was the son of wealthy Christian parents. One day in church, he heard the saying of Jesus: 'Go, sell all you have and give to the poor and come and follow Me,' as a commandment addressed to himself. He withdrew from an ordinary Christian society about 269 AD, and later he went further and further into the solitude of the desert. St. Anthony died in 356 AD at the age of 105 and he is still regarded as the 'father of monks'.

Upper Egypt - Coenobitic (communal) monasticism. In a less remote part of Egypt, the break with society took a different form. Tabennisi in the Thebaid, Abba Bakhomious (290 - 347) became the creator of an organised monasticism. These were not hermits grouped around a spiritual father, but communities of brothers united to each other in work and prayer.

Nitria and Scetis - Groups of ascetics at Nitria, west of the Nile delta, and at Scetis, forty miles south of Nitria, there evolved a third kind of monastic life in the 'lavra' where several monks lived together, often as disciples of an 'abba'. Nitria was nearer to Alexandria and formed a natural gateway to Scetis. It was a meeting place between the world and the desert where visitors, like John Cassian, could first make contact with the traditions of the desert.

Syria - The Egyptian monks created a culture of their own; they made a break with their environment and formed new groups to which the relentless round of prayer and manual labour was basic. In Syria, however, in the area around Edessa and Antioch, and especially in the mountains of Tur 'Abdin, the ascetic movement took a different form. The Syrian monks were great individualists and they deliberately imposed on themselves what is hardest for human beings to bear. Their most typical representatives in the fifth century were the 'Stylite' saints, men who lived for very long periods on the top of a pillar. The first to adopt this way of life was Simon the Stylite who lived for forty years on a fifty-foot column outside Antioch.

Asia Minor - In Cappadocia, where a more learned and liturgical monasticism developed in the heart of the city and of the Church, the key figure was St. Basil the Great. He and his followers were known as theologians and writers rather than as simple monks of the Egyptian type.

Palestine - The great monastic centre in the fifth century was Palestine. In the Judean wilderness, and especially around the desert of Gaza, there were great spiritual fathers in the Egyptian tradition: Barsanuphius and John, Dorotheus, Euthymius and Sabas. The essence of the spirituality of the desert is that it was not taught but caught; it was a whole way of life. It was not a secret doctrine or a predetermined plan of ascetic practice that would be learned and applied. The Desert Fathers did not have a systematic way; they had the hard work and experience of a lifetime of striving to re-direct every aspect of body, mind and soul to God. That is also what they meant by prayer: prayer was not an activity undertaken for a few hours each day, it was a life continually turned towards God.

Abba Agathon said, "Prayer is hard work and a great struggle to one's last breath"; and there is the story told by Abba Lot:

Abba Joseph came to Abba Lot and said to him: 'Father, according to my strength I keep a moderate rule of prayer and fasting, quiet and meditation, and as far as I can I control my imagination; what more must I do?' And the saintly father rose and held his hands towards heaven so that his fingers became like flames of fire and he said: 'If you will, you shall become all flame.' For Abba Arsenius, this was a rule for the whole of life: "Be solitary, be silent and be at peace."

The Hermit Fathers withdrew from ordinary society and sought the solitude of the desert. This was the first step in their 'spirituality'. Then they placed themselves under spiritual fathers. After that, the daily life was their prayer, and it was a very simple life: a small stone hut or cave, a reed mat for a bed, a sheep-skin, a lamp, a vessel for water or oil. It was enough. Food was reduced to a minimum, as well as sleep. They had a horror of extra possessions: "A disciple saw a few peas lying on the road and he said to his father, 'Shall I pick them up?' but the elder said in amazement, 'Why? Did you put them there?' and he said, 'No.' 'Then why should you pick them up?'"

The monks went without sleep because they were watching for the Lord; they did not speak because they were listening to God; they fasted because they were fed by the Word of God. It was the end that mattered, the ascetic practices were only a means.

For the Hermit Fathers, (who have progressed from the community life of the monastery, to solitude in the wilderness), the aspect of warfare with the demons was a major concern in the desert. The desert itself was the place of the final warfare against the devil, and the monks were 'sentries who keep watch on the walls of the city'. Monks were always meeting the devil face to face, and once the great Abba

Macarius asked the devil why he looked so depressed, "You have defeated me", he said, "because of your humility"; and St. Macarius put his hands over his ears and fled.

The knowledge of how to deal with the passions was learnt slowly, by long, hard living, but it was the great treasure for which men came to the desert from the cities. It was this aspect of warfare with demons that was called 'ascesis', the 'hard work' of being a monk. "Abba Pambo came to Abba Anthony and said: 'Give me a word father,' and he said, 'Do not trust in your own righteousness; do not grieve about a sin that is past and gone; and keep your tongue and belly under control...'"

About prayer itself they had little to say; the life geared towards God was the prayer; and about contemplation, who could speak? Abba Arsenius prayed on Saturday evening with his hands stretched out to the setting sun, and he stayed there until the sun shone on his face on Sunday. The usual pattern was to say the psalms, one after another during the week, and to intersperse this with weaving ropes or palms, sometimes saying, "My Lord Jesus Christ, have mercy upon me." The aim was 'hersychia', quiet, the calm through the whole man that is like a still pool of water, capable of reflecting the sun. To be in true relationship with God, standing before Him in every situation. That was the angelic life, the spiritual life, the monastic life, the aim and the way of a monk. It was life oriented towards God.

The lives and the contemplations of our holy Hermit Fathers may help towards a valid interpretation of the Gospel in our own day; their words and their actions may come alive in contemporary life, whatever the particular setting.

A short glossary of terms is included at the back of this book, and for this we are grateful to Father Daniel Al-Antouny for his advice and suggestions. In addition to this, we must mention that the most accurate translation of the Arabic word "El Souah" is "Anchorite, the Spirit Born", however, we chose to remain with the word "Hermit" because it is more commonly recognised. Our interpretation of "Hermit" which has been used for the purpose of this book, is "one who has reached a very high level of spirituality, where his spirit is heavier than his body because he is fervent in spirit and he rarely eats. He is one who can move from place to place in a very short time, without anyone seeing them." It was once said that 'the more the body grows, the more the soul becomes weak, but the more the soul grows, the more the body becomes weak'.

In preparing this translation, we are conscious of our very great dependence on other people: Father Abanoub Attalla for his patience, time and generosity in revising this book, and Priscilla Juste for her constant encouragement and enthusiasm.

The dedication of this book to all our Orthodox monks and nuns who have struggled diligently in the life of monasticism, expresses a debt which must be felt by the whole church to those who have done so much to kindle within us the life of prayer and quiet contemplation, and thereby restore the dimension of the hermit life today.

With such a 'cloud of witnesses' this book should be better than it is and its defects must be laid upon our own shortcomings and limitations.

Lisa & Mary

PROLOGUE

This book is an account of the virtuous asceticism and admirable way of life of the holy and blessed wilderness fathers. They are meant to inspire and instruct those who want to imitate their heavenly lives, so that they may make progress on the way that leads to the kingdom of heaven. The holy fathers who were the initiators and masters of the blessed monastic way of life, being entirely on fire with divine and heavenly love and counting as nothing at all that men hold to be beautiful and estimable, trained themselves here below to do nothing whatever out of vainglory. They hid themselves away, and by their supreme humility in keeping most of their good works hidden, they made progress on the way that leads to God.

Moreover, no-one has been able to describe their virtuous lives for us in detail, for those who have taken the greatest pains in this matter have only committed to writing a few fragments of their more admirable deeds and words. They did not do this to gain praise from men, but only to stir up future generations to emulate them. And now, let us delight in the lives of the fathers which are sweeter than honeycomb (Ps. 19:10), and let us live according to the vocation the Lord has given us and so gain His kingdom. Amen.

AUTHOR'S INTRODUCTION

"In the name of the Father, the Son, and the Holy Spirit, one God, Amen..."

"So He Himself often withdrew into the wilderness and prayed" (Luke 5:16)

Our great teacher and Lord Jesus Christ, taught us to always be on our guard, and through His blessed example, showed us the beauty of the life of prayer and praise in the quietness and peace of the wilderness. Also, John the Baptist lived in the wilderness until the time in which he was to preach God's word to Israel.

Abba Paula the hermit lived in the Eastern Wilderness for eighty years before meeting Abba Anthony, and thus our church gives him the title The First Hermit. Abba Anthony, after returning to his monastery, declared to his disciples, "I consider myself nothing, for I have seen someone who is much greater than I..."

The hermit fathers desired greatly to be with our Lord Jesus Christ, and for this reason, they left everything belonging to the world; putting to death all worldly desires and possessions. They lived in continuous prayer, day and night, until their minds and thoughts became one and united in Christ. Even the bitter grass of the wilderness which they fed on, became as sweet honey in their mouth.

Paul the Apostle spoke of these hermit fathers, "of whom the world was not worthy. They wandered in deserts and mountains, in dens and caves of the earth..." (Hebrews 11:38)

Every soul that desires to grow in the love of our Lord Jesus Christ, is anxious to know about the hermit fathers who constantly taste and live in Godly love.

This book is divided into four sections, containing stories of which history has recorded of our hermit fathers. There are still many more stories, not mentioned in this book, and which no book could be big enough to contain.

May these stories of our blessed Desert Fathers be as a sweet smelling aroma, glorifying our Lord and Saviour Jesus Christ. We ask for the intercessions of our Holy Mother St. Mary, the Hermit Fathers, and all the saints, together with the prayers of His Holiness Pope Shenouda III.

To our Lord be glory and honour forever more, amen.

Fr. Samaan El Souriany
9 February 1986

INTRODUCTION TO
THE HERMIT FATHERS

The hermit fathers have reached the highest level of spirituality and monasticism. They have died to worldly desires and possessions, with the intention of living completely for the Lord who is their every fulfilment and blessing and meaning in life. The Apostle Paul spoke of them saying: "They wandered around in sheepskin and goatskin, being destitute, afflicted, tormented. Of whom the world was not worthy. They wandered in deserts and mountains, in dens and caves" (Hebrew 11:37,38). Such was the life of Elijah the prophet, John the Baptist, Abba Paula the First Hermit, and many who followed. No generation has been and will be without their blessings and prayers.

Hermits are monks who have progressed in their life of solitude. They live in the inner wilderness, in places no one knows, and for many tens of years without seeing the face of a fellow human.

In the life of Abba Bebnoda the hermit, we read how he walked in the wilderness for four days and nights, without having anything to drink or eat, until at last he became hungry. He fed on wild grass, and then continued walking for more than fourteen days; finally meeting Abba Noufer the hermit, Abba Timothy the hermit, and several other hermit fathers. His journey in the wilderness continued for about a month, during which time it was estimated he had walked for fifteen hours a day at five kilometres an hour, thus he walked for hundreds of kilometres within the inner wilderness for the sake of being with the Lord, and meeting the other hermits. If anyone was to search in the wilderness for them, they would neither find them, nor find their way back.

Many of our hermit fathers have spent many years in the wilderness without seeing the face of a fellow human. Such was the life of Abba Paula the First Hermit who dwelt in the wilderness for eighty years before meeting Abba Anthony. Abba Bamon the hermit lived in solitude for sixty nine years without seeing a fellow human; Abba Simon the Stylite, sixty years; and Abba Kara, seventy five years.

Not all hermits have the same pattern of life, however, as some only live a short time in ascetism. Such was the example of Abba Ghaleon the hermit who lived in the Kalamon monastery for many years before desiring solitude, and Abba Misael the hermit who lived in complete ascetism within his cell in the Kalamon monastery. Other examples include Abba Bejimi who resided in the monastery with saintly old monks for eighteen years, yet he humbled himself to the extent that he never lifted his eyes to look into the face of a fellow monk, but kept his head bowed in reverence.

Not all hermits start their spiritual life in a monastery. For example, Abba Paula the hermit started his spiritual life in the wilderness. St. Mary the Egyptian, lived the life of a recluse after her repentance in the wilderness without having joined a convent.

During their life and even at the moment of their departure from this world, God never leaves them, but sends someone to bury their bodies and record their blessed life stories. Our Lord sent Abba Anthony to Abba Paula, to write his story and bury his pure body; He also sent Abba Bemwa to Abba Karas, and Abba Bebnoda to Abba Marcos el Termaki.

These hermit fathers are humans like us who eat, drink and have feelings. Their minds and thoughts, however, are always wandering in spirituality, yearning to be one with our Lord Jesus Christ. At times they may even become absent from the physical world, and be lifted up in spirit toward heaven, just as St. Paul the Apostle mentions "how he was caught up into Paradise and heard inexpressible words, which is not lawful for a man to utter" (2 Cor.12:4). But such revelation is only experienced after relentless struggle in the life of purity and virtue.

The story of Abba Ghaleon tells how he struggled in the life of continuous prayers, being fervent in spirit and exhausting himself in the life of asceticism. He denied all bodily pleasures and comfort, eating only once a week even though he served in the monastery's dining room. He longed for the life of silence and solitude which he found in his cell. There he would find pleasure in reading and meditating on God's word. Thus he lived for many years, until he became old and physically weak, yet his spirit remained strong and eager. He was a hermit who acquired the spiritual treasures of wisdom and holiness which the life of solitude with our Lord produces.

In the story of Abba Misael the hermit, his spiritual father Abba Issac records: "I knocked on his door and after opening he warmly welcomed me. I found his body had become like dry wood, unlike when he first entered the monastery. His hands and feet had become slender like the stem of a palm, and nothing of his body seemed to be left except for his bright eyes with which he kindly stared at me."

Because their minds are uplifted to the Lord Jesus thus feeling spiritual satisfaction, they forget to feed their bodies for many days. David the Psalmist sings, "Thus I will bless You while I live; I will lift up my hands in Your name. My soul shall be satisfied as if with marrow and fatness, and my mouth shall praise You with joyful lips" (Ps.63:4,5). Abba Yohanna Saba (El Sheik el Rohani) says that, "Whoever transforms their mind to the heavenly kingdom will never be imprisoned by anything belonging to the world, for as nothing resembles God, there is nothing imaginable like talking to God...". The hermit fathers do the will of God joyfully with a heart full of love. The Lord lightens their burdens and tribulations, and enables time to pass as quickly as a minute in an hour.

Abba Issac records an experience of one of the fathers who lived his life in a spiritual trance. This father tells us: "I used to stay up praying from the evening to the morning, and then rest a while. Then I would wake to complete my morning duties like someone who is not of this world. Nothing earthly approaches my heart or mind. I spend my morning abiding in the wonder of God's love and mercy. One morning I felt hungry and wanted to eat, after having not eaten for four days, and when I got up to pray before eating, I stood in my cell and the sun was high. I only started the first psalm of my prayer and thus meditated on it until the following day. The sun shone brightly on my face and the cloth I was wearing on my body became warm, and I was not even aware of my existence. When the sun burned my face and my mind recollected, I looked up and found it was the morning of a new day. So I thanked God for His many graces which He grants to those who love Him and call upon Him."

From the time the hermit fathers begin their life of ascetism, they face many hardships and satanic wars. Yet together with St. Paul the Apostle, they "consider the sufferings of this present time not worthy to be compared with the glory that shall be revealed in us" (Romans 8:18). When the Lord Jesus Christ sees their patience, perseverance and their abiding in His love, He grants them His mercy and sends His angels to attend and minister to them. The Lord gives them spiritual wings, so that they may walk and not tire; He makes the bitter grass of the wilderness taste as honey in their mouth and extracts the sweetest water from rocks for them to drink. They lift their hands in prayer and the Lord listens to them. For their sake, the Lord relieves the world of many wars and famines. They talk to God and listen to His voice. Their mind abides constantly in Christ...wandering in heavenly thoughts...tasting the sweetness of Godly love. Such is the life of these hermits who wander in uninhabited mountains, in hunger and in thirst, in cold, hail and heat, and as St. Paul said, "in need, in torment and in pain" (Hebrews 11:38).

- But Your Holy name my Lord Jesus Christ, is their victory in times of trial and tribulation.

- Your Holy name my Lord Jesus Christ saves them in all their afflictions.

- You are the food of life, Who satisfies their bodies and souls.

- You are the spring of life, sweeter than honey in their mouth.

- When they talk about You, their hearts rejoice and their bodies glow.

- When they utter Your name, their minds enlighten and their hearts are uplifted to the heights of heaven.

(Reference to the above are taken from the Annual Epsalmodia and Tuesday's Epsalia)

THE LIVES OF

THE HERMIT FATHERS

1. ABBA KYRIAKOS THE HERMIT

During the times of Pope Benjamin of Alexandria, there lived a righteous man in a village called "Queens Village". This village was later named Tida and was renowned for the sweetness of its natural water.

The Lord enlightened this man's eyes; leading him in the way of solitude. So he arose and went to Pope Benjamin seeking his blessings and advice on the life of solitude with the Lord Jesus Christ. His Holiness prayed on him and directed him to a small cell made of stone beside the sea-shore. Because of its positioning, the cell overlooked the sea and the surrounding countries. The Lord guided and guarded this saint in his life of solitude and isolation, and many people went to visit him in his cell for the purpose of taking his blessings.

In the year prior to the enthronement of the patriarch, an army sent by King Herakel invaded and possessed Syria, and later invaded and assigned a governor in Egypt. The king ordered the patriarch to leave the Orthodox faith or else he would be killed. Accordingly, the patriarch went into hiding. Likewise the Christians were told to deny their faith, or else they too would die. Some, out of fear, obeyed while others obeyed verbally, but not by heart. Great sorrow overshadowed all Christians during this time.

The governor was aware of an ascetic living in an isolated cell beside the seaside, so he ordered his soldiers to find him and bring him back by force. Because of the saint's perfect love and faith in our Lord Jesus Christ, he knew by the Spirit of what was taking place, and after finding him, the soldiers ordered that he believe in the heresy of King Marcoban voiced at the council of Chalcedon. The saint prayed to the Lord to deliver him and protect him from the hands of the heretics and so the Lord listened to his prayer and caused the soldiers to fall into a deep sleep and become as drunkards. The saint was then hidden from their eyes and so when they awoke and returned to the governor, they reported the ascetic was nowhere to be found.

After this incident, the saint arose and ventured into the wilderness to live in and share a cave with wild beasts which rested in it during the heat of the day, and took shelter in the cold of the night. Though wild, they never attacked the saint, but rather, loved him and were friendly to him.

Having not eaten for many days, his body became so weak that he could not stand to pray, so he asked the Lord to provide him with bodily food so that he may have the strength to stand up in reverence and pray. While he was praying for this, a wild cow approached him, screaming as if from pain. The saint noticed it laden with milk, so he took from his cave a shell into which he emptied the milk, and immediately the cow was relieved of its pain. The saint gave thanks to God for His tender mercies, and then drank from the cow's milk. This cow returned to the saint every three days, and the saint fed on its sweet milk for ten years without feeling the need for eating or drinking anything else.

The evil one observed all that was happening and how the saint was growing in spirituality and in the fear of God daily, and he became enraged with envy. For this reason, the devil appeared to him in the form of a frightening beast hoping to distract him from his prayers, but when the saint called upon the Lord and crossed himself, the evil one vanished. Again the devil appeared to him as a vicious beast, wanting to attack him. But the Lord who gives His children power over the enemy, enabled him to overcome through the power of the Holy Cross.

These incidences kept happening for a long time, and so the saint thought to himself, "I must have sinned in the sight of the Lord in this place, and so He must want me to leave this cave and go to another, and I, His faithful servant must do

His will." So he got up and moved to a nearby cave, where again the enemy appeared to him as a hermit dwelling in the cave. The saint was so happy when he saw the old hermit, but was surprised when he neither spoke to him or approached him. The saint thought the hermit to be very holy and spiritual from his many years in ascetism, and therefore did not want to disturb his peace by speaking.

The saint spent the night thinking about him, and as he fell asleep he saw someone in a vision warning him about the old hermit, "for he is the devil who wants to take you away from your Lord. He may have power to fight your body, but he has no power over your soul." The vision then disappeared and the saint woke up suddenly and frightened. He looked around for the hermit in the dark of the night, but could not find any trace of him. Assured that he was the enemy and that he will continue to attack, the saint armoured himself for battle and said, "I will not leave this cave!" As he thought about what had just happened, he heard at the cave's entrance the sounds of galloping horses, and words he could not comprehend. So he went out to look and saw a great number of soldiers all mounted on horses, dressed in black with their faces covered.

They were not looking towards him, so he assumed these soldiers must have lost their way and are undoubtedly looking for their enemies. When one of the soldiers saw him standing at the cave's entrance, he approached the saint: "Man, are you living in this cave?" The saint answered, "Yes". He said, "Tell us then which way our enemies have gone so that we may follow them and destroy them." The saint replied, "I have never seen anyone in this wilderness for as long as I have lived here." The soldier turned to him and questioned, "What then do you feed on?" to which the humble saint responded, "The grass of the wilderness is my food." In a fit of anger, the soldier condemned him saying, "You're lying to me, you know where our enemy has gone!" Having said this, he dismounted his horse, took the saint and tied his hands and feet to a tree which stood in the wilderness, and whipped him bitterly. As he continued beating him, the other soldiers approached him asking, "Why are you punishing this weak man? He has no money and no food to give us." One of the other soldiers came down from his horse and said to the saint, "I will save you from this pain and from this evil soldier, if you tell me where our enemy has gone." Again the saint replied, "I do not know where your enemy has gone." So this soldier, in turn whipped the saint with great hostility.

When they lost hope in him, one of the soldiers took the bound saint and threw him on the back of his horse and rode to the top of a mountain. "Here we will throw you from the highest mountain top so that you may die the worst death, and your body be shredded and eaten by wild beasts!" But when they noticed the saint not responsive, they threw him on the ground and departed. After gaining consciousness, he wanted to return to his cave, but he could not find his way. He then realised that the soldiers were devils whose intention was to fight with humans and lead them into temptation. When he prayed to the Lord and made the sign of the Holy Cross on his face, a path suddenly opened up in front of him, leading him down the mountain to his cave.

As he reached the bottom of the valley, the devil came to him again dressed in black and mounted on a red horse. The saint thought he must be the king's messenger travelling to a far country, and so he wanted to hide from this soldier. But when the evil one approached him he asked, "Why do you try to run from me? I am going to the land of Morocco with a letter from the king and I ask you to show me the quickest way to get there. I will give you food and clothing for directing me." The saint answered, "I am not familiar with direction, for I have lived in the wilderness for many years and have always longed for solitude so that I may lead a repentant life and not die in my sin." So the devil dismantled, took a rope and tied his hands and feet and beat him bitterly. The saint said to him, "You are asking me for something I know nothing about." The devil then threw the saint, bound on the back of his horse with the intention of taking him back into the world and proclaiming, "I found this man in the wilderness, searching for something that should never be (repentance), and looking for precious minerals (gold, which is Jesus Christ)."

The devil's idea was to take the saint out of the wilderness so that he would not think of repentance. But as the soldier was about to leave, the Lord enlightened the saint's eyes, and so he realised it was the devil again; the hater and tempter of the godly. The saint immediately made the sign of the cross, and the devil was swallowed up into the earth with his horse.

After praying throughout the night, the saint finally fell asleep. However, the devil never left him alone. He came to him as a solid wall, tumbling down on top of the sleeping saint. The saint woke up instantly and frightened, but couldn't find anyone or anything because it was so dark. He got up and began feeling the earth and the walls of the cave, when suddenly the devil grabbed his right ankle and aggressively dragged him and threw him about the cave's ground. Distressed over this vicious attack, the saint screamed...but no one answered. After great struggle with this evil presence, the saint crossed himself and at once the devil left him.

One night after he finished praying, he heard a man calling him by the name Pope Benjamin gave him: "Kyriakos, beloved of God, get up and follow me!" The saint thought to himself, "That's strange, I have never heard a voice like this before." So he arose and went to see where this voice was coming from. At the entrance of his cave, he saw a man resembling an angel with two wings. The saint said to him, "You disturbed me and worried me from my sleep; I do not want to follow you, perhaps you are the devil who tempts and destroys humans; depart from me!" and at the sign of the cross, he found him no more.

Another time when he went into his cave at night to pray, he knelt on the ground and stumbled on a great, black, cold body which felt bigger and more fearful than a dragon. It clung to the saint's neck, and he tried to lift up his head to scream, but could not. In his encounter with this beast, the saint realised that it was an evil presence, and so pleaded with the Lord to save him from it. God at once answered his plea by sending His angel to save the saint and cast out the beast.

In all his trials, God was testing this saint's faith and patience, and when He knew the purity of his heart and his faithful and devoted love towards Him, He strengthened him and saved him from the evil one.

Look my friends to what extent this pure saint suffered from Satanic wars, and consider his patience, love and faith in Christ Jesus in overcoming the enemy..!

Our father Abba Benjamin the Patriarch said, "I have often wondered about this recluse and what God has done with him. I prayed that God might reveal to me whether he was alive or not."

On the Sunday following the resurrection, I, Pope Benjamin, was praying in St. Mark's Cathedral church in Alexandria, when I noticed a monk dressed in worn out clothes, entering and standing in one of the church's corners. Immediately I told one of my disciples, "Go quickly and stand near that weak man!" I also ordered another disciple to go with him, "Don't remove your eyes from him for a moment, or else you won't find him!"

When the Pope finished the mass, he asked his two disciples to take the monk to his cell. On arrival the Pope greeted the saint, but did not recognise him. When food was brought to him, he pretended to eat, but didn't. The Pope noticed this and when they were alone, he asked him, "Saintly father, where did you come from and where are you going?" The saint did not have the heart to hide anything from the patriarch, so he answered, "I am your son who dwelt in the cell in Tida and Efragon, and you are aware of all that had happened to me during that time. I have since been living in the wilderness." The Pope lowered his eyes to the ground and cried, "Bless me Father Kyriakos, for I glorify the Lord who allowed me to see you again, and thanks be to God who heard my prayer, and did not turn me away from Him, for I have asked of Him to reveal to me whether you are alive. Please bless me!"

I asked the saint to tell me all that had happened to him, and so he revealed all. I asked Isezoros the writer to record the story of this saint, as it was told. Abba Kyriakos stayed with me for three days before returning to his place in the wilderness. He told me God revealed to him that after four months, he will die in his cave, so I made note of his hour of deliverance to Paradise, and as the day approached, I directed Simon the bishop of Rasheed, and Tidor the bishop of Atreeb and Khael the bishop of Dimyat to go to the place instructed to them. I sent with them a guide to lead the way, and gave them food, drink and horses for transportation. Isezoros the writer and deacon also accompanied them on the journey to attend the saint's departure and bury his pure body.

Along the way the devil appeared to them as a wild beast charging forward to attack them. From fright, they lost their sense of direction, but the saint saw them from afar frightened and lost in the wilderness and so he came forth and comforted them. When the saint took them into his cave, they told him all that had happened along the way. The saint explained to them that this beast was the devil; the one from whom he had had many trials...

The saint knew by the spirit that these fathers were sent to bury his body after departure, so they remained with him for two days. On the third day, this pure, beautiful saint passed over into the Paradise of his fathers the saints. The bishops buried him with great reverence, and in a manner instructed to them by the Patriarch.

Isezoros the writer, who wrote the life story of Abba Kyriakos, as I Pope Benjamin told it, added to it what he saw and experienced during the time of the saint's departure, and the wonders which were revealed when his spirit departed his precious body.

Glory be to the Father, to the Son and to the Holy Spirit now and forever, Amen.

2. ABBA JOHN THE HERMIT

Abba Alos said: There was once a father called John, who dwelt in the wilderness. He was a great, spiritual elder and surpassed many in his ascetism and virtues. No one could ever search for him in the wilderness, as he constantly moved from one place to another. In the beginning of his solitary life, he spent three years in continuous prayers and only slept a little while standing. One of the priests used to bring for the saint the Holy Communion every Sunday.

One day the devil came to him as a priest and brought along with him a woman. Immediately the saint knew it was evil and said, "You full of deceit and the enemy of the godly, you have no power over me, nor over the faithful, for the Lord crushes you and your power under our feet!" After pausing, the devil answered him, "Soon I will have power over you and conquer you!" The saint rebuked him in the name of Jesus, and he immediately vanished.

It happened at one time that the saint's legs became very dry, swollen and oozed pus and water. The angel of the Lord appeared and said to him, "Do not fear, the gift of the Holy Spirit which enables you to partake of the Spiritual Food will be sufficient for you." And after healing him, the angel advised him, "Leave this place and go into the inner wilderness." So at once the saint went forth and fed on the shrubs of the wilderness, but every Sunday he would return to his old cave to partake of the Holy Communion.

Once there was a paralytic who had heard of the spirituality of this saint, and earnestly desired to see him, so that through his prayers he may be healed. Because of the greatness of this man's faith, the saint knew of his situation, and without having seen him, the man's legs were immediately strengthened through the grace of God and the prayers of Abba John. Likewise another man that was paralysed was also healed through the prayers of the saint. We thank God and praise His Holy Name, and ask for the prayers and blessings of His saints.

May the blessings of Abba John the hermit be with us Amen.

3. ABBA STEPHANOS THE HERMIT

In the wilderness of El Fayoum:

Listen my friends and I will tell you what I witnessed with my own eyes and heard with my own ears...

One day, I was wandering in the wilderness and meditating on its valleys, mountains, and many wild beasts which become tame to humans. So I gave thanks to the Lord...

As I ventured through the wilderness, I noticed many different trees and springs. Under one of the trees I found a skull which had turned white from the extreme heat and cold of the wilderness climate. I glorified the Lord and wondered who this skull belonged to and what life that person lead. I wished it had a tongue so that it could reveal to me what it is now experiencing.

I looked towards the east and prayed to God, asking him to reveal to me its secret. Before I had finished my prayers I heard a voice calling, "Father Stephanos, listen to me and remember my words for it will be a warning to you and your brothers. Warn them about the fearful judgement day; woe to those who don't pray and are not vigilant, for in the great day of the resurrection of bodies, no brother will defend his brother, nor father his son, but faithful work and mercy will bring one closer to God. Prayer lightens up brightly like a lantern, so beware and do not tarry. Tell my words to all in the hope that they will learn and so avoid coming to the place where I am; in torment and unquenchable fire and restless worms...

My story is that I was a greedy merchant and even though I had a lot of money and treasures, I envied everybody and never gave money to the poor. I had no mercy on anyone and never prayed. Nothing I did pleased or glorified the Lord.

I had good sons who loved all people and carried out many acts of love and mercy. They advised me to do well, but I refused to listen and thus did not give them access to my money. But despite the fact that I had great possessions, I was never satisfied with what I had...

One day I travelled to a distant country, for the purpose of trading. I took camels and servants, and was prepared to spend time during my journey in an oasis. I hired a guide for direction and took lots of money and goods for trade.

After one day of travelling through the wilderness, the guide lost his sense of direction, and so for three days we roamed about the wilderness, not knowing where we were going. Woe to him whom God is not his leader! The morning heat was scorching, so the camels died, the servants escaped and I was left alone. The love of worldly possessions and luxuries prevented me from seeking shelter in a cave, so I stayed for three more days eating from the food remaining, until there was nothing left. I felt as if I was about to die, and I was very disturbed at how quickly life was disappearing considering I had done no good deeds to save me, and I had no power to raise myself up out of my present misery.

The next day, my eyes became heavy, so that I could no longer see, and on the third day my eyes opened, and I saw a very frightening angel, holding a sword of fire and from his mouth he breathed fire. He ordered my soul to leave my body, and after grabbing it, he gave it to the devil. So they stabbed my soul with a fork and brought me to this place of torment where I was thrown and left alone...

I saw in the bottomless pit an old man whom I knew in the world and his deeds were just as bad as mine...he too was being tormented. I asked him for what reason he was cast here, and he said, "My terrible deeds..." Suddenly I heard great thunder which no one on earth could bear hearing, and there he was, the angel in charge of torment. He grabbed me and cast me into Hades, where I remain until this hour." I Stephanos asked him, "Can you see those in Paradise?" He answered, "No one can see them, for between us and them is an immeasurable distance. Woe to me and that hour when neither money nor possessions nor children saved me... So take heed to my words Father Stephanos, never delay to do good or pray, and alert all people to my words.

I was always disobedient to my parents, and a lover of worldly desires. I never lived according to the commandments, and never had faith in Jesus Christ, even though I knew all along that the Lord who came into this world was incarnated of the Virgin Mary, and was resented by His own. I knew that through faith, the Holy Baptism and the sacrament of Holy Communion one could be saved, but because of my pride, I refused to abide in them. Never neglect these gifts!" He repeated these words three times and said, "I have been ordered to speak these words to you!" Then he ceased to speak.

I, Stephanos, took the skull into the cave, dug a hole and buried it. I then went to my brethren and told them all the things which took place. Together we prayed and asked the Lord our God to make us worthy to live in obedience, according to His will; to live in the hope of eternal life with our Saviour Jesus Christ, which has been promised to us after the resurrection of the dead.

To Him is everlasting glory, amen.

4. THE FEMALE HERMIT

Slash, a saintly father from El Balkaa, was sitting in a cave near the monastery of Faraa, not far from the 'Holy House of God' (Bate el Mokadas - Jerusalem). All the brethren were gathered around him as he told the story of his close friend the hermit, who lived in the cave of El Kalamon:

"I used to visit him on all festive occasions to receive his blessings and give him food. During the feast of the Jewish Passover, I took with me some bread, and went out as usual seeking the saint's cave. To my astonishment, however, I could not find it. I was very sad, and kept wandering downheartedly in valleys and hills until the scorching sun made me very thirsty. I pleaded with the Lord not to prevent me from seeing His saint...

Suddenly, I noticed human footsteps in the sand. I rejoiced and recognised them to be either the footsteps of a young boy or a woman. So I followed the footsteps until I saw weaved straw covering what seemed to be a cave. I moved it aside, giving way to the small entrance of a cave. I did not want to enter without permission, so I called out, "Bless me, my father the saint!" No one replied, so I quietly entered. I saw a monk sitting in silence, so I approached...and we spoke a little. I perceived him to be a eunuch because of his small frame and delicate features. He asked me to pray, but I declined, asking him for his prayers and blessings. He replied, "You are a priest and therefore you must pray, father!" I tried to hide this fact, but he said "...and you are not allowed to lie!" After praying, we sat down together, and I thought to myself, this person is either a eunuch or a woman. The hermit quickly responded, "Why are you thinking so much about me?" I was amazed at his insight, and so fell down before him. He raised me up saying, "You must promise me that you will not reveal my identity and my story to anyone until my hour of departure has come, please, for the sake of the Spirit that dwells in you, you must not tell anyone...Father, I am a virgin. I was the daughter of an aristocrat from Constantinople. My father insisted that I marry his friend, also an aristocrat from Constantinople. I never agreed to this, nor did I reveal to my father my intentions. Many times I would sit alone and pray to my God to help me depart from this passing world.

When the time came and he wanted me to marry, I said to him, "Father, in the first place I have promised God to go to His Holy House in Jerusalem and pray there, please do not forbid me, lest I take punishment from God Himself." He equipped me for my journey with horses, servants, maids and 3000 denarii with which to distribute amongst the holy churches and monasteries. I arrived at the Lord's house in Jerusalem, and after praying, I left there a portion of my money.

During my trip I visited many Egyptian marketplaces, but my most uplifting experience was visiting the caves of the saintly fathers. There were three elders who lived in these caves; one of them I noticed was clothed in sackcloth. I rejoiced exceedingly, for I was looking for a monk who would keep my secret and clothe me in the holy 'eskeem' of monasticism (monastic habit). As I thought about this elder in sackcloth, I said to myself, "He is the one who abides in God's love and will..."

When our trip was coming to an end and all our gifts had been distributed, we remained an extra four days in the holy city (Jerusalem) before preparing ourselves for the journey back home. I then sat down and wrote two letters : one to my father and the other to the guide who was with me on the trip. In them I expressed my desire to give myself completely to the Lord, "...so do not try to find me, as I will go to the place my God will lead me." After this, I said to the guide, "I want to pray in the Church of the Holy Sepulchre, and in Golgotha before returning home."

After Golgotha, I said to my maid, "Stand here." I then quickly escaped from the town through Jericho and went seeking for the elder in sackcloth. When he saw me he was puzzled, and so I assured him, "I have left all that is in the world and belonging to the world in order to be alone with my Lord, and I have come to you so that you may dress me in the holy 'eskeem', as this is my wish." I gave him all that remained with me - money, jewellery and clothes. When he saw my many repentant tears and my earnest desire, he got up, shaved my head, dressed me in the holy 'eskeem' and clothed me in a garment made of loofa plant.

The next morning, I got up early to pray before leaving. When the elder realised this, he said, "Where are you going?" I answered, "Wherever God leads me, through your prayers, father." He prayed on me and gave me spiritual books for nutrition. Then I left...

I rejoiced saying, "I have surrendered my soul to the Lord Jesus Christ in this blessed wilderness, by the prayers of this saintly father..!"

The Lord has guided me to this place and ever since, I have been living in this cave, rejoicing and giving thanks to the Lord. I was then eighteen years old when I met the elder in sackcloth, and today is my twenty eighth year of asceticism, and you are the first human I have seen within this time."

Her face was shining brightly like the rays of a sun and when she had finished what she was saying, I asked her to eat from the food I brought. She did not accept and said, "If I eat from the food which you bring, who then was feeding me all these years?" When I heard this, I sighed for my many sins, and I asked her to bless my food, which she did in simplicity.

I asked her not to depart from her place until I come to take her blessings once more. We prayed together and then I left, praising God. Amazingly, during my journey back through the wilderness, I did not feel thirsty at all until I returned to my cell.

After a few days, I returned once again to her cave, but did not find her...it was not God's will.

Glory be to God.

5. Abba Khristozolos the Hermit

My dear friends, there once lived in the mountains east of Egypt, near the Red Sea, an ascetic who fed on the weeds of the wilderness and drank rain water. He was brought up in Christian love, in the Egyptian town of Aen Shams. Despite the fact that he held a very good position, he left everything in the world to dwell alone in the mountains with the Lord. This is his beautiful story...

When he was still living in the town of Aen Shams, a woman who served the Arabs came to him. She was very beautiful and had asked him to make her a pair of gold earrings. She remained in the town until he had finished her earrings. As they discussed the price, she approached him saying, "O man, do you not know that whenever a man sees me, he desires to have me?" She continued trying to entice him, but the man casted his eyes towards the ground and replied, "I have no doubt that you are the daughter of the chief of devils, for he is the only one who could manipulate you this way...I do not want your money, nor do I ever want you to return to this place again. Now leave, from now on you shall never see my face again." At once, he thanked the Lord for His grace and mercy, and immediately got up and returned home.

He began blaming himself saying, "Woe to you my soul from the frightful day; are you going to lead my body as well as my spirit to the eternal fire? Realise now, my soul wisdom and goodwill and walk in the way of salvation. O my soul awake! things in life are either harmful or beneficial. Harm comes from disobedience, and benefit comes from obeying the commandments of God. O my soul, do not tread upon the paths of the ignorant and blind, and if you want to move to another place, let it be a more honourable home than the one you have at present so that your pleasure in the Lord may increase, for whoever sows thorns labours in vain, but whoever sows palm trees eats from its fruits. O my soul, look at the saints who left the world to live alone with the Lord in the wilderness, like Abba Anthony, Abba Macarius, Abba Bakhomious, and many others...So run away from the world now and you will be saved!"

When he had finished this meditation, he distributed all that he owned. His father had died earlier and left his possessions to the mother. Most of these possessions were given to the poor, and the rest was kept by his mother who brought him up in righteousness and the fear of God. He advised his mother to continue in her faith and good works and said to her, "As God wills, I desire to go the Eastern Mountain to live in peace and solitude with the Lord Jesus Christ, for this world and all that is in it, is in vain and will pass away!" He farewelled his mother and left immediately, venturing towards the mountains, having taken with him enough food and water for three days.

When God knew the purity of his heart, He enabled the saint to arrive at the place chosen for him, in less than a full day's journey, but because of the simplicity of the saint, he did not even realise God's intervention.

From where he was situated, he could see the sea and its terror, and after praying, he spent the night there, as he was exhausted from walking. In his sleep he saw someone saying to him, "You who loves the Lord, get up and look!" And immediately he got up and saw three men dressed in white garments and leaning on rods engraved with crosses which shone as bright as the sun. He quickly got up to greet them and one of them approached him saying, "My dear son, where did you come from, and what are you doing here?" He replied, "I have come from the town of Aen Shams to dwell alone with the Lord in the mountains. I am a stranger here, and therefore not familiar with directions." So they asked him, "Would you like to accompany us and be one of us?" Anxiously the man replied, "Yes, for the lost stranger must walk with he who dwells in the house, if he is wise. I can see that you are the beloved and obedient of God, walking in His way, and this has been revealed to me by these beautiful, shining crosses on your rods." They said to him, "Walk behind us and follow, but do not tarry!"

He followed them until the morning, when they reached a beautiful garden which seemed like paradise. They said to him, "Stretch out your hand and cut for yourself a rod, and then stretch out your arm and take for yourself a cross to put on your rod, for God has chosen you because of the purity and goodness of your heart, for your strong faith and your willingness to obey Him." Immediately he cut for himself a rod and found many crosses of diamonds, from which he took and placed on his rod. When he had done this, he lifted up his head and found himself alone, so he wept. He did not know who they were or where they were from, or where they had gone. He did not even get the chance to ask them about themselves or seek their advice about his new life with the Lord, and so he wept bitterly for many days.

Eventually, he realised that they will not be returning to him, so he got up and walked in the beautiful garden. He found the grass sweet to taste, and the water delicious to drink, so he thanked the Lord. At night he would seek shelter in a cave, and the crosses on his rod would brighten up like beams of light leading him to his cave. Whenever he leaned on the rod, the Lord would shorten the distance for him to walk.

He lived for many years in the garden, feeding on its grass which tasted like honey in his mouth, and drank from its sweet rain waters. He protected his body from the heat of the day and the cold of the night by making for himself a covering from the bark of trees...

When the enemy saw the saint living in such a beautiful garden, and greatly cared for by the Lord, he was enraged with envy, so he at once approached an evil group of people who were his followers and would not disobey his orders. He appeared as a man from the West and told them, "Dwellers of the wilderness, get up and come with me for I will show you a hidden treasure which I cannot steal without your help!" Anxiously they got up and followed him on horses, taking for themselves food and water. The devil lead them to the saint's garden, and when they saw it they rejoiced and exclaimed, "The treasure must be hidden in this garden which is in the care of that young man!" The devil pointed towards the saint, but when they tried to approach, the saint and the garden were hidden from their sight. All that was revealed to them were high mountains, but no clear path leading to the garden. It is evident therefore, that this garden was only for those who were pure in heart, and those who pleased the Lord by their deeds; and thus He rewarded them.

These evil men remained on the mountain for three days during which time all their food and water had finished. They became distressed when they could see the fresh springs and the fruitfulness of the garden, but could not reach it. The enemy then approached the saint in a frightening figure and stood at a distance saying, "You are not a worshipper, you are not merciful, you are not even obedient to God, and you are not a friend to strangers, as the Commandment says, for can't you see those men thirsty but have no water to drink? Get up at once and serve them, so that you will achieve the blessing and reward from God and forgiveness of your sins!" The saint thought these words to be from God alerting him, so he arose and went to the men, taking from them a container and filling it with the sweet water from his garden. But when they followed him back to the garden, something prevented them from entering and the garden was hidden once more from their sight. The evil men then turned to one another and said, "This man must be from God..., let us get up and leave this place quickly, before the wrath of God comes down on us..." One of these men had a garment and offered it to the saint because he saw him naked and only clothed in tree bark, but when the saint refused to take anything from them, they left, and so the enemy's plan was in vain...

They returned to the rest of their group and told them all the things they saw. They spoke about a righteous man who lived in a beautiful garden which no one could enter or approach without the saint's permission. "We found him to be a lover of God and he kindly gave us water to drink from his garden. We remained in the mountains for three days, during which time we never tasted water so sweet, as the water from the saint's garden!"

But the devil never rested...This time, he took another group of his followers, disguised them to look like saints and lead them to the garden. When the saint noticed that they never prayed, nor mentioned the name of our Lord Jesus Christ, nor looked towards the heaven, the Lord directed his thoughts in righteousness and by doing the sign of the cross on them, they immediately fled. So the saint praised and thanked the Lord.

Abba Khristozolos lived in solitude for many years in obedience to God and away from all worldly desires. He willingly accepted his new life with Jesus Christ, forgetting the world and all that belonged to it.

As the Lord revealed to him that the hour of his death was soon approaching, the saint asked the Lord to send on the day of his departure, the three fathers whom he met in the beginning of his life in the wilderness, so that they may pray on him and bury his body. As he was thinking about the three elders who came to him that night, leaning on rods with beautiful bright crosses, he suddenly heard a voice calling him, "The Lord has answered your prayers and has sent us to you so that you may tell us your life story and it shall be shared and told to others too..." As the saint told his story, one of the elders memorised it by heart, and when the hour had come for the saint's departure, the elder asked his fellow wilderness dweller to write the story and send it to his home town of Aen Shams.

The saint's birth name was Alian, his father's name was Youstos, and his mother's name was Kalmana. His birth town was Aen Shams. This beautiful saint had accomplished his Christian struggle on earth, and had passed away on Tuesday the 10th day of Abib, in the peace of God who preserves us all in His love.

To Him is all glory, honour and worship now and forever, Amen.

6. THE HERMIT IN THE GLASS MONASTERY

Abba Boctor, the writer and abbot of the Descendants Monastery, commonly known as the Glass Monastery in the city of Alexandria said : "Listen my beloved brethren and believers of the Lord Jesus, I shall tell you what I saw with my own eyes!

At the age of twelve, I greatly desired monasticism and so came to the monastery where I lived with a saintly man who used to write spiritual books. He gave me the best education and teachings and eventually I became a writer too. The Lord enlightened my heart and eyes and I accepted his teaching with great love. Many years after my teacher died, I became the abbot of the monastery, much against my will as I loved to live the life of solitude.

When I became abbot, I found it very difficult to find time to write despite people asking me to write many books. As a result they approached the Patriarch and requested that he replace me as abbot so that I may dedicate more time to writing. I loved to write the stories of saints, especially those I met.

One day while I was meditating upon the many wonders of the saints; their struggle and their victory over the devil, I looked out of my cell window and I saw a monk walking hastily towards the monastery. His clothes were very worn out and when he approached the monastery, I viewed him closely. He seemed very tired and leaned against the wall of the monastery to rest a while. I quickly said to one of my disciples, "Go down to the monastery and bring that monk to me!"

The monk greeted me and together we sat down. I asked him about his story; where he had come from and where he was going. He answered, "I have lived in the wilderness of

Saba for several years now and I want to receive the Holy Communion and see my saintly fathers, before I die. In my sleep last night, I had a vision of someone telling me, "Get up and hurry to the Descendants' Monastery (the Glass Monastery), for you shall see there, the saints whom nobody knows about; see them, receive the Holy Communion and know that after ten days, you will depart from this vanishing world to be with your Heavenly Father in His home. The saintly fathers will pray on you and bury your body..."

I got up immediately, seeking this place though I did not know the way, but when I began to walk, I heard the voices of people talking, and so I turned around to see three men dressed in white carrying in their hands censors full of incense. They were praying and giving praise to the Lord and they lifted up their heads towards Heaven hourly one after the other. I was overwhelmed by the beautiful sight and praised God. I approached and asked them to pray for me; so they blessed me. I asked them where they were going and they answered, "We are going to the Descendants' Monastery."

I followed closely behind them, and within a short time, we arrived at this monastery. We sat at the door for a moment to rest and I did not even notice anyone opening the monastery door, but when the three elders entered and I followed, they disappeared from my sight. I was very puzzled." Abba Boctor then said to the monk, "I saw you coming forth out of the wilderness, but I did not see anyone with you." When I Boctor turned towards the saint, I could not look into his face as it resembled the face of an angel, so I glorified God.

I then took the saintly father and went into the church as it was time for the Holy Mass. He received the Holy Communion, and later we returned to my cell. When I offered him food to eat, he said, "I have not seen food for many years; my food is the grass of the wilderness and I drink rain water." He then took out some grass and ate from it, "This is sufficient for me for a week." He also gave some of it to me and I ate it. He stayed with me for seven days, telling me the stories of the hermit fathers in the wilderness, of those who eat from the grass of the wilderness. I asked, "My saintly father, I ask you for the sake of the Lord Jesus Christ to pray for me so that He may lead me on the path of righteousness and humility so that I will never have need for this earthly food." He smiled saying, "If you would like to come with me, then come along."

I found it difficult to walk because I spent most of my life sitting down in order to write holy books, and also because of the weakness of my faith. The hermit father said, "Ask and you will be given, seek and you will find, knock and it will be open to you, for whoever asks will take and whoever seeks will find and whoever knocks it will be open for him" (Luke 11: 9-10). He then said, "I shall go now, but later I will return to you." In less than three hours he returned and brought with him more of the wilderness grass. I was touched by the purity of this saint's hands and heart and how he pleased the Lord with his simple deeds.

I was thinking about what the hermit father had said earlier, about having only ten days left before departing to the Eternal Home. Eight days had already passed. On the ninth day he said to me, "I wish, my saintly brother, that you bury my body when I die tomorrow and bury my bones with my fathers the saints." I asked him, "Please tell me, where are the bones of those saints?" He warmly smiled saying, "Boctor the writer, do you not yet know? Get up and come with me." So I got up immediately and followed him. He walked me to the outside of the monastery and I saw tombs I had never seen before. I saw saintly fathers coming forward to greet him and pray on him. I stood watching from a distance and heard one of them saying to him, "We are waiting for you to come and be with us..."

As I heard their beautiful voices, I could not lift up my eyes to look at them or ask anything of them. I then heard voices praising and singing triumphantly, "Holy God, Holy God Lord of host, heaven and earth are full of Your glory and honour!" I turned and lifted up my eyes but could not see them, I found the saintly hermit father had passed away and was lying on the ground. Woe to me from that hour! How can I bury his pure body? How can I make for him a tomb like these other tombs belonging to the saintly fathers? I approached and kissed him and there I saw beside him a grave already dug. I carried him carefully and placed him within, then left wondering about the story of this saint and the many blessings the Lord has bestowed upon him because of his patience, faith and peace.

I went back to my cell and told my brethren the monks what I saw. They rejoiced when I told them about the place of the saint's tombs. When I took my fellow brethren to the tombs, so that they could take their blessings, I became disorientated and could not remember nor find the saints' tombs and so I became quite confused. My eyes were weak from ageing, so I ate from the grass the saint had given me and immediately my sight became stronger and I was able once again to continue writing holy books...

I wrote this story so that the believers might know the extent of God granting grace to those who follow His commandments and do His will, without allowing anything of this world to touch their heart, for this world with its deceit and desires can cause some of the chosen to fall. Therefore take care my brethren to please the Lord by being obedient to His will so that you may be found blameless on the day of judgement and thus achieve the kingdom of heaven.

Glory be to the Father, to the Son and to the Holy Spirit one God forever, Amen.

7. ABBA ZAKARIA THE HERMIT

Abba Jacob once said: When I was still a monk in the monastery, before being ordained bishop, I wanted to go to the town of Tarnot to visit one of my fellow brethren. I took a rod in my hand to support me while walking, and around midday I felt thirsty so I stopped for a while and drank from a nearby river. At the river I saw three barbarians who had seized a man who was trying to cross over. They stripped the man of all he had, took his horse and tied him up wanting to kill him by drowning him in the river. I watched them from a distance so that they could not see me and when they were about to kill him, I raised my voice and shouted loudly. They thought I was one of the governor's soldiers manned with an army, and so being terrified they jumped into the river. As it was the season for high tide, they all sank as they clung together, until they were seen no more.

After this incident I sat alone and thought to myself, "Today I left my cave and saw this disturbing scene. It was because of me that these men have drowned. Perhaps later in their lives they may have repented but it is my fault for preventing this." It only occurred to me after this incident, that what happened was a lesson from God to show me the fate of a sinner.

I approached and untied the man telling him to take only his belongings and leave immediately for he was saved from death. I did not know which possessions belonged to him, but it was obvious that the love of the world had consumed his heart because he wanted to take all that belonged to the three barbarians as well. We were both heading towards Tarnot and although he was walking alongside me I did not ask him where he was from or where he was going. On the way I spoke to him about the devil's traps and enticements but he refused to listen.

When we reached Tarnot, he took out the sword which belonged to one of the barbarians, and went into the market place to sell it. A man quickly approached him and asked, "From where did you get this sword?" He replied, "It belongs to me, I bought it and now I'd like to sell it." But the man grabbed him and said, "I want the man from whom you bought this sword, for it belongs to my brother who has now been missing for the past six days and I do not know what has happened to him. You must have killed him and then taken his sword!" He then took him to the governor telling him that, "This man has killed my brother and has taken his sword!" Witnesses also validated this after recognising the sword and seeing the robber could not justify himself. The governor then ordered that the robber be beheaded by the stolen sword. The news of this event spread throughout the town, however, I Jacob, was still uncertain as to whether it was the same man or another. Taking with me my fellow monk, we went out and saw this same man being bound hands and feet awaiting to be beheaded. Quickly I went to the governor pleading, "May God preserve your life for I have something I would like to tell you..." As he patiently listened to my words, I told him my eyewitnessed account and story of this man, and the governor was greatly amazed. Accordingly he then ordered that the man be released once all the stolen belongings are returned to the barbarians' relatives.

Thus this man was saved in the first place from being slaughtered and drowned and secondly from being beheaded by a sword he had stolen. After this final incident, the young man approached me saying, "My father the monk, I would like to repent to God and leave this world, in order to be your son." I answered him, "My son, you cannot live the life of monasticism and solitude for no one can live this life unless he is patient, denies all worldly desires and practises prayer and fasting. He loves all people and pleases God by his good deeds. He does not keep company with the evil or exalts himself with the proud..."

After teaching him the traditions and rites of monasticism he still insisted on a solitary life, so I said, "Get up my son, and beware of laziness because it leads to sin." As the three of us (including my fellow brother the monk) returned to the monastery, I wondered about this man, who he was and how old he was? I left him behind with the monk from Tarnot, asking my fellow brother to take care of him and teach him prayer and fasting.

Our new brother had the responsibility of keeping watch at night and guarding the monastery door. He was a strong and healthy man and in his new life his deeds were pleasing to God. Thus I dressed him with the holy 'eskeem' of monasticism, and daily he diligently increased in virtues and prayer and fasting.

One night as he was praying, the enemy of goodness, the devil, came to him in the appearance of his father (as his mother had already passed away). He approached the saint saying, "My son, Zakaria, I have worked hard for your sake all my life and I thought you would at least support me now in my old age. So what has hardened your heart against me and why are you living alone? I am now an old man and I have no one but you; I want to give you all the money and riches that I have, lest someone else takes it from you." The devil was so deceiving that the saint believed this message to be true.

The next morning, Zakaria came to me asking, "Father Jacob, I need to go to Tarnot to see my father and be assured of his health; and I shall return after three days. I would like to ask for your permission as I have not seen him for the past three years and during my prayers, he appeared to me saying, "I want you to come to me and take my money which I have left for you, lest someone else takes it, for I am dying..."

I the weak Jacob, realised at once that this vision was from the devil, who had become envious of his new life of worship. Therefore I advised him not to go to Tarnot. That same night, the devil came to him again repeating what he had said previously. Once again the saint asked for permission, but when I refused, he thought I had selfish intentions and so he disobeyed me and left on his own accord.

When he arrived at Tarnot, he greeted his father who asked him, "My son, why have you left the monastery and your pure life of solitude?" The saint answered, "It was you who drove me out of the monastery!" He told his father about the two visions, to which his father replied, "My son, I have not left this house for the past year; I do not know what you are talking about, for I do not even know the monastery where you abide." The saint at once realised that it was the devil who came to him and encouraged him to leave his monastery.

When he returned to his cell, he locked the door and wept bitterly for allowing himself to be enticed by Satan's deception. He wept for many days until his heart was purified from all evil thoughts. On Palm Sunday, he came to me after prayers and said, "Father Jacob I would like to say goodbye, and I ask you to pray for me, for I would like to go to The Holy House in Jerusalem to pray there and by the will of God, I shall return quickly." I replied, "My son, there is no way you can make it, for there are only five days left before Easter." But he refused to listen.

After honouring his wish, I saw three men standing waiting for him so I held him and asked, "Son, who are those men?" He answered, "They are monks from the monastery of Saint Macarius the Great; we are going together because they know the way." He did not take with him food nor money in his belt, nor shoes on his feet; but clothed himself in worn-out wool. I farewelled him and watched as the four of them ventured off together. I did not know what will happen during their journey nor what would become of him; undoubtedly the three monks are saints but as for this brother, he had not yet reached their level of spirituality.

After the glorious Easter, I the weak Jacob, went and entered his cell where I found three gigantic dragons. When they tried to attack me, I quickly escaped. I heard a voice shouting, "Jacob!" three times. I thought these beasts were from the devil, so I glorified God, blessed His Holy name and made the sign of the cross on my face. The dragons came forth rolling on the ground, and I heard a voice saying, "The monk who was living in this cell, used to bring us food and drink, and now it is seven days since we have had anything to eat or drink. You are the abbot of this monastery, how is it therefore that you do not know about us?" I said to them, "God willing, I will provide for you all food and drink." After doing this, I then warned the brethren from approaching Brother Zakaria's cell.

On the tenth day, the three monks from Abba Macarius' monastery returned. I quickly went up to them but hesitated to ask about my son Zakaria, as he did not return with them. They began telling me stories of the beautiful City of Jerusalem and I wished so much to one day go there. Within myself, I wondered how these fathers walked to Jerusalem and back in such a short time!

From the time my son left me to venture with the three fathers from the monastery of Abba Macarius, I had not heard from him or about him.

Following my ordination as priest, I the weak and unworthy Jacob, was ordained a bishop and as I was standing in the church on the day of my ordination, I saw my spiritual son and his three friends present. No one else could see them but me and I was astonished about this. After the celebrations, I ran out to greet them, but sadly, I could no longer find them so I said to myself, "Why did I do that? I must have driven them away!"

When I entered the sanctuary, they were standing before me and after the reading of the Holy Gospel, they approached the Iconostasis and I heard them proclaiming, "Lord have mercy!" three times. They received the Holy Communion and quickly left, while I stood entranced watching them. I told the priests who were with me in the church, to hurry up and catch those monks, but regrettably they could not find them. I wept bitterly because I did not have the chance to talk to them.

In the evening I headed back to my cell in Oseam where I saw four men facing eastward praying. I stood at a distance watching and wondering who they were, as I noticed they were dressed in monastic habits. I took a lamp and went towards them, and as the light shone on their faces, I recognised them to be the blessed fathers and my spiritual son. I rejoiced exceedingly and quickly brought them food to eat. After eating, they bid me farewell, and left glorifying the Lord Jesus Christ, who alone is worthy of glory, honour, dominion and worship with His gracious Father and the Holy Spirit giver of life,

Now and forever and ever, Amen.

8. ABBA MOUSSA THE HERMIT

In the vast wilderness of Sheheet, there lived an ascetic monk in the valley of Habib. Living for the glory of Christ alone, he denied all worldly pleasures and humbled himself to be clothed in weaved palm branches. He spent his time in fervent prayer, patiently tolerating the heat of the day and the cold of the night. Satisfied with only small portions of food, he ate only once every few days, and he kept watch of the time by observing the moon.

God was pleased with his pure heart, and so lead him to a garden of olive and palm trees. He would eat from whatever fell, according to his need, and happily drank rainwater. Because of his gentleness, the beasts became his friends and loved him. When it was time for his prayers, he would cross himself, and immediately the beasts would leave him in peace.

The beasts felt that this man was a man of God and one year when there was an awful drought, all the animals gathered together outside his cell and screamed as if to beg the saint to pray for rain. Also, if any of the beasts were ill, they would approach the saint, as if to ask for his blessings, and they would immediately be healed...for thirty five years the saint lived in peace and complete harmony with the beasts in the wilderness... but the enemy was not far away.

The devil envied the saint's patience and his friendship with the beasts of the wilderness, and so said to himself, "How could such a human overcome me, me, the mighty and evil one of fire and light. I must make him obey me!" Immediately he appeared as a very old monk, with long white hair, bare-headed and dressed in sackcloth. Supporting himself by a rod in his hand, he walked slowly, from one valley to the next, but never stopped to pray. Watching from afar, the saint wondered about this old ascetic who should well be accustomed to prayer and worship. As the saint approached him, the devil pretended that his eyes were dimmed from old age and so did not look or speak with the saint one word. They spent that night together and every time the saint uttered the name of the Lord Jesus Christ, in his prayers, or did the sign of the Holy Cross, the old man would disappear. The saint thought that it was because of his unworthiness that God kept hiding the old man from him and every time the saint spoke to him, the old man would not reply. They remained as such for three days...

On the fourth day he answered the saint, "What do you want from me my son the saint, you who pleases God by your deeds; blessed are you for He has prepared a place in His house for you since the beginning of the world!" When the beasts saw this old man, they were all frightened and ran away, so the saint wondered what the purpose of this reaction was. The old man asked the saint his name, how long he had lived in the wilderness, what he ate, what he drank and what he wore? He then said to the saint, "Son, you are chosen of God; so now tell me about yourself so that I may too share my story with you." The saint then began, "Father, I was born in Damshish, Alexandria and my name is Moussa. When I was about thirteen years old, I ventured into the wilderness of Sheheet, where I lived together with a monk in a small cell. He taught me about the beautiful rites and traditions of monasticism. At the age of twenty, I no longer had any regard for this materialistic world, but greatly longed for eternal life. I knew that the path to eternity can only be reached through prayer and fasting and abiding in the Lord and His commandments. So I left everything pertaining to the world, to seek peace and solitude with Christ in the wilderness. Yours is the first human face I have seen in many, many years, but I wonder, are you a dweller from a foreign wilderness? For three days I have known you and have not yet seen you pray. Please teach me how to pray so that I may learn from you and receive your blessings."

The old man responded, "Son, when I was a young man, I had countless wealth, indulged in eating and drinking and hated the poor. I had a passion for adultery and on such I spent all my money. I even stole, lied and envied viciously. I spent many years of my life enjoying these worldly pleasures, until I realised my frightening fate in hells' fire and torment. So I gathered together my belongings and wealth and distributed it to the poor, in search for eternal life. For the past forty years I have lived in Barka. I am sure that God has forgiven me my sins, because when I felt the day of my death approach I asked the Lord to send someone to pray on me and bury my body. I was not familiar with praying or any of the Christian rites and sacraments, for my upbringing was not Christian, but I felt that because I had distributed my possessions to the poor, God was pleased with me, and thus had mercy on me. I dwell in Taouna, one of the five cities in Barka near Alexandria. God had revealed to me your life story and dwelling place, and so I have come seeking you. I have only forty days left before I die, and the Lord has shown me the place where He wants me to be buried. Get up my son and follow me!" Obediently, the saint followed without realising it to be the deceit of the devil, the enemy of righteousness.

As they walked, they saw in the midst of the desert a majestic palace, as if belonging to a king. As the old man approached it, the saint followed closely behind. The palace was surrounded by beautiful gardens and its magnificence was overwhelming. The elder said to the saint, "Come, my money is buried here, so here too you must bury my body, so that you may acquire a large inheritance for yourself. In time, another elder like me will also bury your body next to mine. After ten days I will pass away...beware of the devil for he despises truth and righteousness!"

As the saint approached the palace door, he marvelled over its beauty and its peculiar situation in the isolated desert. Turning, he saw a woman dressed in a royal gown, and so frightened, he stepped back from her. But the old man said, "Take care and listen closely my son, for I shall tell you my reason in bringing you here and what is required of you. If you do not adhere to my words, great sufferings will come upon you, and you shall no longer have the patience and longsuffering to bear the heat of the day and the cold of the desert nights.

This majestic palace was built by my forefathers and it was the home I was brought up in. As I have already related to you, in my youth I was merciless with my wealth and was always hungry for more, until the day I decided to leave this materialistic world to live the life of solitude in the wilderness. However, before having taken this decision, my wife bore a child and said to me, 'she is yours, take care of her.' She died shortly after. I have done my best to bring up my daughter in the best possible way, but as you can see, my daughter is now a beautiful woman, and yet I cannot find her a husband more suitable than yourself. Consider, and do not disappoint me, for when we look at the examples of our fathers Abraham, Issac and Jacob, we learn that marriage is a blessing from God, and is not a sin!" But the saint declared, "Woe to you O my soul, for how can you dare commit such a thing!"

When the saint saw that the old man's hour of death was approaching, he asked, "What do you require of me in your hour of deliverance?" to which the devil replied, "I give to you my palace and all that is therein, I also give you my beloved daughter to be your wife." And having said this, the devil pretended to die. Immediately the saint carried his body to the place instructed and shown to him by the old man, and there buried him. Having done this, the saint then tried to enter the palace, but suddenly he was caught up in a violent whirlwind, which lifted him high and abruptly dropped him on the ground. The saint landed on his back, as if dead...

After he regained consciousness, he did not find a trace of

the palace, and found himself in the midst of the wilderness, not far from his cave. He was extremely angry, and roamed about restlessly looking for food, as he was hungry. He ate from the grass of the wilderness, but its usual sweetness was replaced by bitterness, so he spat it out and threw the grass away. The beasts, who had loved him were now frightened of him. The coldness of the desert night was now uncomfortable for him and he became lost and frightened in the desert. It then occurred to him that this old man was the devil in disguise; the enemy of all mankind...

The saint then said to himself, "Woe to you my soul, woe to you! I beg you dear God to give me time to repent!" Because of his inability to no longer cope with the hunger and thirst, and cold and heat of the wilderness, he got up with the intention of venturing into the world...Again the devil came to him as an old man riding a donkey. Approaching he asked, "Where are you going?" to which the saint replied, "I am going to the city of Alexandria." The old man was delighted at the prospect of deceiving this saint another time, and so eagerly said, "I too am going to Alexandria, come with me and I shall take you there upon my donkey!" The devil's intention was to take the saint as far away from the wilderness as possible, so that he would not have the chance to repent and weep for his sins; for the devil is aware of how merciful God is to those who turn away from sin. The old man gave the saint water to drink and food to eat, and quickly led this lover of God out of the wilderness.

He then took him to a place near Alexandria, called Hala, and told him that this village has an abundance of exotic fruits and produce, including grape vines and fig trees. He also told him that the people of this village were the most hospitable in the entire region. Having said this, the devil departed from the saint. Venturing towards the village, the saint noticed a well from which people were drinking. As he stood watching them, the devil appeared to him, once again, but as a beautiful woman clad in worn out cloth. Upon her bare shoulder she carried an urn with which to fill up with water from the well. She came toward the saint and asked, "Who are you, and where are you from?" The saint replied, "I am a dweller of the wilderness and have come to this village to seek something to eat and drink." The woman offered, "Come, rest in my house this night, and I shall give you food, drink and comfort."

After the saint had filled himself with food and drink, the woman went in to change her clothes, and later emerged in a seductive dress. She approached the saint and said, "I can see on you the signs of repentance, for no doubt you are an ascetic," to which he replied, "Yes, however, I have been deceived by the devil who disguised himself as an old man, for the purpose of driving me out of the wilderness." Intrigued, she questioned him further about this incident, and the saint, having trusted her, revealed all.

The woman eventually brought up the subject of marriage, while telling him her life story. She told him of how she was the king's daughter, and how after his death, she inherited a great fortune. When the saint seemed convinced of her story, she said to him, "One thing I lack, and that is a husband. The only hindrance between us is that I am Jewish, and the daughter of a rabbi priest; therefore, I cannot marry you before you deny your Christ, for in my religion there is no Christ, nor do we know about Christ." Immediately the saint declared, "I will not tolerate listening to you any further, for how can I deny my Lord and Saviour Jesus Christ?" To this she replied, "You will not be the first one to deny Him!" But because of her enticements and deceptions, the saint eventually fell into her trap. She then requested, "I want you to shave your head, cut your nails, and take off your old clothes, for I shall dress you in the clothes of a prince, but only after preparing for you a bath of holy water which has been blessed by my priest..."

Such was the cunning trickery of the evil one over our saint! Later in the evening, the woman said to him, "Get up and follow me, for I shall show you where my treasure is hidden!" She led him into the midst of a vast, frightening wilderness, full of wild beasts...The saint became very thirsty, but looking around, he could not find anything to drink, so she said to him, "Stay where you are; I will go up to the top of this mountain to look for water, and then I will call you to come." He remained waiting for her at the foot of the mountain, but when she had reached the top, she called out to him in a loud voice, "You, O weak and helpless saint who suffered and strived all these years in the wilderness, come, for you have now embraced the devil, for behold, I am one of his soldiers! You have denied your Christ for the worship of my father the devil, who will overcome the human race, for he is the one preventing the Jews from believing in Christ! Woe to you and joy for me! Now I have deceived you and fulfilled my intention of keeping you away from your worship, so that you may die a horrible death in this vast wilderness, for alas, there is no way back!" Having exclaimed this, she vanished.

He looked around, seeking a path to follow, or water to drink, or shelter for his body, but could find none and so he became overwhelmed with fright and anguish...and thought about the trials brought upon him by the evil one. After returning to his senses, he was greatly sorrowful and cursed himself saying, "Woe to you O my soul for you abandoned the path of righteousness and eternal life, to tread upon the road leading to hell and destruction! Woe to you, for you have fallen victim to the passing pleasures of the world in place of eternal riches. Imagine how much riches you have lost! Woe to you my soul, for you have denied the name of your Lord and Saviour! Have you forgotten that He created you and blessed you with a mind, and gave you His Word, so that through understanding you may know what is right and what is harmful? I have disobeyed my God for the sake of satisfying my bodily desires! Woe to you O my soul for neglecting God's kingdom in exchange for vain glories on earth!"

He cried bitterly, and like the righteous Job, exclaimed, "May the day perish on which I was born, and the night on which it was said 'a male child is conceived...' As for that night, may darkness seize it; may it not be included among the days of the year, may it not come to the number of the months. O, may that night be barren! May no joyful shout come from it" (Job 3:3, 6-7). "Why did I ever take notice of that old man and listen to him, for he caused me to deviate from my path of righteousness? How did I ever consider following him? Woe to you O my soul for finding pleasure in the appearance of the palace and the woman who lived within! Woe to me, for I left the wilderness to be led astray and deceived by the trickery of Satan's soldier! Woe to you O my soul, woe to you!"

He lifted up his hands towards heaven and wept, then threw himself to the ground and rolled in the dust. He prayed and cried grievously, "O my Lord Jesus Christ, have mercy upon me, my Lord Jesus Christ, have mercy upon me..!" Then our great, loving and merciful God, looked down from the heights of heaven and heard his pleadings and prayers, and saw the repentant tears of the saint, confessing his sins and declaring his earnest desire to live the remainder of his life in repentance. Our beloved Lord Jesus Christ willingly accepts everyone who turns to Him through repentance.

The Lord then sent His angel to comfort the saint saying, "After three days, you will depart this vanishing world to be united with your Heavenly Father and the whole host of saints and angels, and I will send to you Abba Samuel, whose deeds are well pleasing to the Lord, and he will pray on you and bury your body." Having said this, the angel then departed from him.

As the saint gazed into the vastness of the wilderness, he saw in the distance a monk coming towards him. Immediately he got up and ran to the monk and fell at his feet saying, "Father, God has been merciful to me and forgiven me my sins, and has accepted me to once again be His child!" In joy of God's love, they embraced each other, then blessed and prayed for one another. The saint then told the monk all that had happened to him, and how the devil never left him...at the palace...in the wilderness...at the well... And the saint revealed all...

Abba Moussa then confessed to Abba Samuel the monk, "From the time I first dwelt in the wilderness, during the leadership of Pope Benjamen of Alexandria, to this present time, I have not had Holy Communion." At once, Abba Samuel, a monk-priest, said to him, "Get up my son and follow me."

After having walked a short while, we came to a beautifully built church with doors that were open wide. There was no one inside, so we entered and prayed. Abba Samuel then turned to me and asked, "Do you know this place?" to which I replied, "No my father, I have neither seen this church nor known about it before." He looked at me with warm, gentle eyes and said, "This church is usually reached only after a ten day walking journey through the wilderness..." As he was saying these words, a group of saintly fathers came into the church, lit all the church lanterns, and dressed themselves in the beautiful, bright vestments for celebrating the Holy Mass. The priest offering the Korban (Holy Bread), was Abba Samuel. Together we all shared in this glorious occasion in partaking of our beloved Lord's Body and Blood.

After the Holy Mass, I quietly asked Abba Samuel, "Father, who are these people?" To which he replied, "Each of these fathers live a solitary life in the wilderness, but on this day each year, they gather here to celebrate the Holy Mass and receive the Holy Communion. They meet here in this church which was built by the righteous King Aghabious, who reigned over the five cities of Alexandria. He was a strong believer and lover of our Lord and Saviour Jesus Christ, and so all the people used to come regularly to this church to pray. However, in time the sins of the people became great, and therefore the Lord hid His blessed house from their sight and revealed it to the saintly desert dwellers so that it could be their home and burial place. But it is better that you not concern yourself with anyone or anything other than God Himself."

Abba Moussa then asked me, "Father Samuel, please show me the place where the saints' bones are buried." I led him to the revered place, opened the door for him and watched him enter. He knelt down and rested his forehead on the body of one of the saints in order to receive his blessings. After tarrying there awhile, I called out to him, but there was no response. I approached him and found that his soul had departed his pure body. I carefully covered him, took his blessings, and walked out locking the door behind me.

I went back to my place and began writing his life story. I the weak Samuel, have written and recorded this story in my own handwriting in Greek and have given it to a fellow believer who was travelling through an oasis. I have requested that he take this scroll and place it in St. Mark's Cathedral in Alexandria, for all people to see how much this saint suffered from the trials and tribulations of the devil, but how God was merciful and loving to him because of his fervent prayers and repentance. In this blessed story, I have also mentioned the church in which Abba Moussa had passed away, so that it may be remembered forever.

Glory, honour, blessing, praise and worship are due to the Father, the Son and the Holy Spirit, now and forever more, amen.

9. MAR OLAG EL SABAII, THE HERMIT

Born of righteous parents, he was brought up in a family with strong Orthodox beliefs, and as the Lord says, "a tree is known by its fruits." The grace of God enlightened his mind and so he left this world with all its vain glories and desires to live in a monastery with saintly fathers. He remained there a few days before venturing into the wilderness seeking the cave of a righteous solitaire called Isezoros. This saintly man abounded in spiritual virtues and was filled with the love of God. The elder accepted the young saint happily and found for him a cave beside his own.

After testing him, the saint found him to be obedient in all his doings, and felt that he will be a chosen one of God. When Isezoros knew the purity of this young man's heart, he clothed him in the 'eskeem' of monasticism, and strengthened him in his spiritual life. As a result, the saint would fast with a smile; being silent, obedient and humble in all things and towards his spiritual father Isezoros.

When the evil one saw the young saint increasing in virtues and the grace of God daily, he was enraged with anger, and sought to make war with him, but all in vain, for the love of God, and the prayers of his spiritual father, enabled him to overcome all trials and emerge as a victorious knight.

Within a few years, he became so filled with the grace and spiritual strength of his spiritual father Isezoros, just like Elisha the disciple of Elijah the prophet. He would fast diligently without food for ten days, then feed on the grass of the wilderness. He would spend the night in vigil with his hands outstretched towards heaven, just like a cross, and when he would feel the need to rest he would lean against the wall and sleep awhile.

For these reasons, Satan was afraid to approach the saint as he would sit in his cave enjoying God's presence and heavenly visions. As for Father Isezoros, he became very old, yet because of his spiritual struggles and hardships, God gave him the strength to conquer Satan to the last moment of his life. He knew by the Spirit that it was time for him to go to the place where, "eyes have not seen, or ears have heard, nor has entered into the heart of man, the things which God has prepared for those who love Him" (1 Cor.2:9), and because of his great love for our Lord Jesus Christ, this saintly father was indeed worthy of these heavenly graces.

He called his spiritual son Mar Olag to him and said, "My beloved son, I have served the Lord all my life and have taken care of my temple, and with the help of God, He has given me strength to conquer all evil powers. God will not reveal to us His hidden secrets if we are not purified from our sins; as the Apostle has said, "You are the temple of God and the Spirit of God dwells in you" (1 Cor.3:16). So be pure my son, both in body and heart, and be without deceit, and our Lord will fill you with His infinite love and glorious light. Show humility in all things and be prepared, for one day you will accompany a saint called Mar Okeen who is the head of a group of saintly fathers, for the Spirit of God has called him to spiritually shepherd this group of saintly fathers, and by their prayers the worship of idols will be abolished from all the lands of the East, and all people will fall down to worship the Lord our God. You too will have a great inheritance, for God has chosen you."

Having said this, he looked towards heaven and released his soul. With joyful praise the angels carried it to the Paradise of delight, where it rested with all the saints. Sweet smelling incense surrounded Father Isezoros' body, indicating the departure of a blessed soul to be united with the Heavenly King who glorifies His saints.

God then began to reveal His holy will, for, "a lamp cannot be hidden under a basket." Mar Olag was of ill health, but this was God's will. Not far from the saint lived many lions; one of which became a close friend of the saint; even a disciple, serving the saint and never leaving his side. When the lion saw that the saint was ill, he went roaming the mountains until he found a shepherd shepherding his flock on the mountain side. The lion lead him to the saint, and pointed to him as if to say, "See what the saint needs." The shepherd was very frightened and fell down kissing the saint's feet saying, "Have mercy on me and save me from this lion, because it will obey whatever you order it to do!" So the saint answered, "Do not be afraid, for God because of His mercy ordered the lion to bring you here to me. Please, bring me some water." The saint drank two mouthfuls and rested awhile, due to the severity of his pain. The shepherd then said to the saint, "If my goats were nearby, I would have brought you some milk to drink and cheese to eat." But the saint answered him, "I have many goats", and the shepherd assumed he was talking about goats like his own.

The saint offered the shepherd some of the fruits of the wilderness to eat. After they ate, they glorified God saying, "Blessed are you O God for giving sweetness to these fruits for the sake of your saints!" The saint then prayed for the shepherd and asked, "Would you like to return to your goats? Do not worry, they are safe, for I have sent seven lions to care for them." The saint then ordered his lion, "Take this shepherd back to his goats." The lion immediately carried him on his back and took him to the place where the goats were being protected by the seven lions, just as the saintly father had said. So he glorified God.

The shepherd at once went forth into the city to tell his townsfolk about all that had happened, and anxiously they all sought the saint's cave to receive his blessings and prayers. The pure saint knew by the Spirit that this is God's will, and so he came out of his cave to greet each one and bless them.

He gave them figs as a blessing before they returned joyfully to their homes, praising God.

Seven years had passed since the death of his spiritual father Abba Isezoros, who prophesied that Mar Olag will one day be in the company of the saint Mar Okeen. He thought many times on how he would reach the town of Keetis to meet the saint Mar Okeen. One morning, he looked up and found the lion in his cave. It had taken the Bible, placed it in a bag, hung it around its neck, then went out and stood in front of the cave. The saint was astonished and felt that it was God's intervention. The lion then entered once again, took hold of the saint's tunic and pulled him out, so the saint was then assured that it was God's will. The lion lead the saint to the town of Keetis, where he found Mar Okeen with a group of fathers. When they saw Mar Olag they were very happy and ran to greet him. Looking at his face, the fathers noticed it was full of light, like the face of an angel, and the lion remained accompanying and serving the saint, so the brethren called him 'Mar Olag of the lion'. The lion loved all the brethren and harm never came to any of them.

When Mar Okeen and his disciples entered Antioch, they found three high priests secretly offering incense to idols; for King Constantine had ordered for the destruction of all pagan temples and forbid the worship of idols. Mar Olag went to meet the three priests and the lion stood in front of them so that the priests could not escape. The saintly father then began preaching to them about the word of God, and the glory of His infinite love. He prayed for them and remained with them for six days, until the Lord had heard his prayers and enlightened their eyes, hearts and understanding to the Truth. Immediately they repented and implored to the saint saying, "We believe in your God and in His Son Jesus Christ, please pray for us so that God may forgive us our sins." And so God willingly accepted their repentance.

The saint then took the three men to a nearby spring, made the sign of the cross three times in the name of the Father, the Son and the Holy Spirit and then baptised them. He said to them, "Get up my beloved, go to Egypt and ask for the monastery of Abba Bakhomious, and there be consecrated as monks." They obeyed him at once and ventured off in search of this hallowed place, where they were to be ordained as monks and clothed in the holy 'eskeem' of monasticism. These three new fathers lived for many years in solitude and spiritual struggles, before departing to the place of eternal rest.

The news of the saint went throughout all the land, and many would seek his cave in order to ask for his prayers and blessings.

Once they brought to him a man who had become mentally, physically and spiritually ill from his many dealings with the devil. The saint knelt on the ground before God and prayed fervently with tears, then anointed the man's possessed body in the name of Jesus Christ. The man was immediately healed, and left glorifying God.

There was a woman from the town of Batana who was severely possessed by the devil. When they brought her forward towards the entrance of the saint's cave, the devil screamed, "I will not enter the cave of this man who torments my kind!" Once again the saint anointed her with holy oil, and at once the devil left her exclaiming "Woe to us from Mar Olag the Copt!"

Another time, they brought to him a barbarian woman who was demon possessed. They remained outside of the cave's entrance because the lion would not let anyone enter. After three days the devil came out of her screaming, "I cannot remain in a place where Olag of the lion is, for he destroys our work!"

A barbarian man had been blinded by the devil which

possessed him, so he went to the saint's cave and remained at its entrance for six days; during which time the Lord had cast out the devil and restored his sight through the prayers of the righteous saint Mar Olag.

A young girl from Alexandria was brought to the saint, bound by two iron chains due to the severity of the devil within her. After three days of being with the saint, she was healed by the grace of God and by the prayers of Mar Olag.

There was a young girl from Halab whose body was covered in ulcers, because of the devil which had possessed her. She and her parents suffered greatly because no one could dare look at her. When they took her to the saint, he took his cross, washed it in water then gave it to her parents saying, "Anoint her body with the cross." After doing this, she was immediately healed through his prayers.

A man from Bethsaida lived all his life in adultery. He went to the saint begging for his prayers so that he may be released from this sin. On the third day, the saint allowed him into his cave, and this sinful desire was lifted from him.

There was a man from Antioch called Tara, whose hands and feet were so dry that it was impossible for him to walk. After three days of being with the saint, he was healed.

There was a man called Simon who had a daughter whom he loved dearly. Because she was so beautiful, the neighbours envied her and wanted their son to marry her. When her father refused, the daughter was so infuriated that she became possessed. The saint, by the Spirit, had already known her story, without being told, and so he prayed for her throughout the night. In the morning she was completely healed and so they knelt before the saint, kissed him and left praising and glorifying God. The story of this wonderful miracle spread throughout all the country.

One day the saint was walking in the wilderness and stopped to rest within the shade of a tree. The lion went off wandering in the mountains and returned to the saint followed by a donkey carrying food and drink, and accompanied by a shepherd. When the shepherd saw the saint, he knelt before him and said, "Bless me master, for this donkey is mine, and I have felt that the Lord used this lion to lead us to you so that we may give you something to eat and drink. Please, I ask you to pray for me." The shepherd told him about his goats which had leprosy and asked the saint for a blessing to give to the goats. When the shepherd returned to his flock, he put the blessing which the saint had given him, in the water which the goats drink from. After drinking from the water, the goats were healed and they shed new fur.

The saint went to the town of Balsi and met Mar Okeen and his brethren. They rejoiced on his arrival, and together they ventured into the wilderness. The lion was with them, and as it was roaming the mountains, it found a young boy upon a donkey, carrying loaves of bread. The lion pulled the donkey by the rope and lead it back to Mar Olag. On arrival, the saint found that the young boy had died from fright of the lion. The saint cried and lifted up his hands towards heaven and asked Jesus Christ to raise up the child. The Lord answered his prayers and the soul of the young boy returned to him. As they talked to each other, the father of the boy came seeking him and when he saw the boy, he hugged him and cried, "Two days I have been seeking for you in this wilderness!" The saint said to him, "Your son was found dead in the wilderness, but we prayed to the Lord to raise him up, which in His infinite love He did." The man asked for the blessings of each of the fathers, then left with his son. When the townsfolk heard of this story, they all glorified God, and all those with various diseases were cured, through the blessings of the saint.

A few days later, the saint and his disciples went down to the River Euphrates, where they crossed over to the town of Nassiben. There they built a church and caves for shelter. Some of them preferred to seek shelter in the shadow of trees, and others on the mountain sides. Wherever they were, they carried out the work of angels.

Mar Okeen then took them to the shores of the Tiber River, where they preached to the people and performed many miracles, until the worship of idols ceased. Accordingly, they returned to the wilderness with exceeding joy.

Mar Olag was requested to go to the town south of Nassiben. The region was surrounded by four neighbouring towns which were active in the worship of idols. The lion accompanied him throughout all his journeys. One day he went into each of these four towns, and after doing the sign of the cross on each of the pagan idols, they crumbled to the ground. Although the people feared what had happened, they persisted in pursuing their sinful ways, and so rebuilt the idols. God's wrath came upon the people and so they became very ill and their bodies were covered in ulcers. They gathered together and said, "These gods of ours have no power, or else they would have healed us, instead we are suffering excruciating pain. Let us go therefore, and search for the saint Mar Olag and he will be able to heal us by his prayers..."

When they found the saint's cave, the lion allowed them entry, so they said amongst themselves, "This man must be from God, or else the lion would not obey him so." They asked the saint to pray for them and lead them along the paths of righteousness. He gathered them together with the people of the four towns and began preaching to them about our beloved Lord Jesus Christ. He healed them of their illnesses, and after they repented and declared their faith and belief in the Lord, he baptised them in the name of the Father, the Son and the Holy Spirit.

Mar Olag's Last Days:

The saint longed for the life of solitude in the wilderness and had no desire to live in the company of fellow human beings. The Lord answered his wish and said to him, "My beloved Mar Olag, you are to remain in this wilderness for the rest of your life..." The saint rejoiced and gave thanks to God. He continuously prayed for the safety of the church and her children, to whom he preached the faith.

One of Mar Okeen's disciples strayed from the faith and began sowing the seed of pagan worship. At this time, Mar Olag appeared to three pagan priests in a dream and said, "Why have you left your Orthodox faith and accepted the deceit of magicians who worship the devil? Come to me tomorrow and bring with you Mar Okeen's disciple." When the three priests awoke, they gathered together all the aristocrats and magicians of the town and told them what they had seen in their dream. They took along with them Mar Okeen's disciple who said, "I will prove to you that it was Mar Olag who caused us to stray from the faith!" When they approached the saint's cave, the lion jumped on Mar Okeen's disciple and tore him into four pieces.

The blessed Mar Olag departed to the Heavenly Kingdom on the 10th of Abib. He was one hundred and twenty years old when he died, and he was ten years old when he first entered the monastery. The lion had served the saint for forty years, and after Mar Olag's departure, the lion kept guard of his pure body which lay in his cave. Many came to take their final blessings and be healed of their ailments.

Forty days after his death, God instructed the fathers from the monastery of Mar Okeen to bring the body of the saint. Two hundred ascetic fathers gathered together, headed by Father Andras. When they came to Mar Olag's cave, the lion licked their feet and wept. Carefully they carried the body of the saint. The hair on his head, and his beard were down to his waist, and when the lion roared loudly, all the people of the town came. There were twelve thousand men in all.

Gabriel, the man whom the saint had healed from leprosy thirty six years earlier, brought with him a beautiful tunic in which to clothe the saint's body. As they carried him away, the lion accompanied them. In the crowd was a man with one eye who in complete faith, approached the saint's body asking for his intercessions. Immediately God gave him sight, and so he glorified the Lord who honours and glorifies His saints.

They placed Mar Olag's body in the sanctuary and fasted for three days. After this time, they took him to the cave of Mar Okeen and dug within, a grave to rest his holy body. Three days after Mar Olag's burial, the lion which had accompanied the saint for forty years, died. Father Andras ordered the brethren to dig a grave and place the lion within it.

To our Lord be glory and honour, now and forevermore, amen.

10. QUEEN ANNASIMON, THE HERMIT

St. Annasimon was brought up in her father's palace as one of the royal children. When she was seven years old, a righteous priest was requested by the king to teach and show Annasimon the fear of God. He read for her stories of the saintly hermit fathers, monks and solitaires, and the way they cast out devils through the power of God.

Earnestly she began reading their life stories, with a secret desire to one day live the life of these saintly fathers. She much preferred to read the stories of saints than engage herself in royal pomp and ceremonies.

The life stories of these hermit fathers touched her heart in a remarkable way. Under her dress, she wrapped her body in Hessian material, and she forbid herself from indulging in exotic food. But no one else in the palace was aware of this. She wanted to escape to a monastery, but she feared her father. Confused she cried bitterly day and night, lifting her eyes towards the heaven saying, "My Lord, You know the secrets of my heart, so please ease the way in which I must go, so that I may do Your will." She prayed continuously and gave away to the poor whatever came to her from her father's palace, like food, fruits and goods, and she preferred to eat dry bread and salty cheese.

The Lord knew the purity and faithfulness of her heart, and how she greatly desired to do His will. Her mother had already passed away and when her father, whom had ruled over seven provinces died, Annasimon became deeply saddened. All the army commanders and soldiers gathered together and decided to crown the king's daughter Annasimon queen on her father's throne, so that the kingdom would continue to be stable and be prosperous.

This honour was much against her will...

All the people of the town, the priests, the bishops and the patriarch, and all the rulers of the kingdom gathered together to celebrate her enthronement. The church fathers prayed on her, and all the people rejoiced saying, "Blessed is he who comes in the name of the Lord!" There was joy and happiness in the land like there had never been before.

She was very beautiful, and when she sat on her throne all the people obeyed her. To her was given mighty fortresses and majestic castles. She released all those who were enslaved and imprisoned in her kingdom. She gladly gave away money and possessions to monasteries, widows, orphans and to the poor. She remained steadfast in her praying and fasting and never forgot the most precious thing in her life - our beloved Lord Jesus Christ.

A year had past since her enthronement, then one night she said to herself, "Annasimon, the Lord Jesus Christ has given you all that your heart desires, and you have achieved and fulfilled all your aspirations, therefore, what reason is there now for you to continue living in this world with all its passing pleasures and vain glories? If you earnestly desire to attain the Kingdom of Heaven, get up and prepare yourself now. The Lord has given you strength and free will, so do not waste any time. Do not let this world and its lustful desires deceive you and take you away from the joys which are prepared for you in God's heavenly kingdom. Haven't you read what He has said in His Holy Bible, 'Whoever does not carry his cross and follow Me is not worthy of Me'?"

Immediately she got up with the intention of fulfilling this commandment. She removed her crown and said, "My Lord Jesus Christ, it is because of Your great love for me that I leave this kingdom which I have inherited from my father and grandfathers." She then dressed herself in an old outfit which belonged to one of her servants. She knelt at her bed three times and farewelled it saying, "The Lord be with you until His will be done." She then covered her head and went out barefoot. She stood for a while at the front of the house and looked at the beauty of her palace for the last time and said, "I leave you in the care of Christ." Approaching the palace door, she knelt three times and kissed the ground saying, "Open the door of Your mercy O Lord before me, for You know my nature; I am a woman and a weak vessel, so please don't ever leave me. Be my helper and protector, for I know no one but You." She took her Bible and the small book containing the stories of monasticism and the hermit fathers, then she crossed herself and left the palace grounds quickly, heading towards the wilderness, out of Constantinople.

It was a dark, cold night, but the angel of God protected her. She knew not where she was going, but in the morning she saw that her feet were bleeding from walking so much, and she rejoiced at her new suffering. The enemy began to frighten her concerning the dangers of a woman travelling through the wilderness at night on her own, but the Lord eased her fears. When she became hungry, she ate of the grass of the wilderness, and continued to roam day and night without any direction, and without seeing a fellow human being.

When the beasts sighted her, they approached her and became her desert friends. She awoke to their sound early in the morning, and they kept her company until late at night. The Lord provided for her a palm tree and when she would eat of its dates, she would wet the stones until they became soft enough for her to eat. She then thought to herself, "When they want to fatten cattle, they feed them these wet date stones; woe to you my soul, for you have left your ruling over people to become queen over beasts of the wilderness!"

Later, she thought to herself, "I will get up now and go to a convent and serve in its most lowly places, and I will tire for God's sake and be patient in times of abuse and trial."

She walked until she arrived at the door of the convent, and she appeared to them as a mad runaway. When the gatekeeper saw her, she ran in and informed the Mother Superior. Annasimon, for the sake of not being over welcomed, pretended to be mad when she saw the mother approach her with a group of nuns. She kept stepping back from them as if from fear. The nuns said, "Look at this poor one; she is crazy!" They mocked her until they were able to catch her, and then dragged her into the convent. Not knowing what to do with her, they gave her the responsibility of cleaning the bathrooms, but whatever Annasimon was ordered to do, she did it with dedication and enthusiasm.

Still pretending to be mad, she would snatch a bowl of soup whenever she became hungry, then slept on the ground. The nuns constantly wondered about her, and the more they wondered, the more she continued in her pretence.

One of the monastery fathers questioned the Lord Jesus Christ on the various levels of spirituality, and so the Lord revealed to him many saintly fathers, but declared, "None of these fathers have reached the level of spirituality of St. Annasimon the queen, who left her kingdom, and her power to humble herself in appearing as a mad woman before many..."

When he heard this, he marvelled and sought the convent where it was revealed she dwelt. On arrival, the nuns ran to take his blessings, then lead him to Annasimon. When he looked at her, he saw a crown of light upon her head, and on her body, a heavenly garment. The nuns, not having seen this revelation, said, "Father, keep away from this woman, for she is crazy!" But in humility he turned to them and said, "I am the crazy one, the poor and the ignorant. Open your eyes and look at this pure saint and great queen!" He then took her by the arm and the saint trembled. He said,

"This is Annasimon, the queen and ruler over seven provinces. She left her palace open for all and sought the Lord Jesus Christ with all her heart. My beloved Lord has revealed this to me and has said that no saintly father has reached her level of spirituality." When they heard these words, they wept and fell at her feet screaming, "Forgive us O pure lady!" They continued pleading with her all through the night. When they fell asleep, Annasimon opened the convent gate and quietly escaped. In the morning when then awoke, they could not find any sign of her.

One day while a priest from the city was in his church resting, he awoke to the beautiful aroma of incense coming from the sanctuary: "I hurried and opened the door of the sanctuary and found a person standing in the midst, praying. I looked about and found all the church doors closed, so in fear, I trembled and fainted. The person then took my hand and lifted me up saying, "Do not be frightened", and called me by my name. This in turn made me tremble even more. The person then said to me, "Hurry and get for me a little flour and wine in order to make the Holy Bread for Holy Thursday, which will be celebrated by four hundred fathers." I asked him, "Where are all these fathers?" and he answered, "It is not for you to know these places; just take their blessings by doing as I ask." After giving him the flour and wine, I begged him saying, "For the love of God, please take me with you so that I may see these saintly fathers." But he answered, "You do not need this." When I persisted he said, "On this same day next year, wait for me and I will come to you again." He then farewelled me and left.

I waited anxiously for a year, and on the same day at the same hour, while I was again resting in the church, I awoke to the sweet smelling incense. I ran to open the door of the sanctuary and found the same person standing there praying. I threw myself at his feet and said, "Bless me my master!" and so he blessed me and I kissed his hands. I asked him about the fathers and he replied, "they are praying for you." I then said to him, "You have promised to take me to them." But he answered, "It is better for you if you do not come with me." I pleaded with him, "Father, for the love of God, take me with you!" Again he declined, "It is not the time now, just give me the blessing of flour and wine so that I may prepare the Holy Bread for Holy Thursday's mass." I did as he requested, but felt very sad, so he said to me, "Next year, double this blessing and wait for me outside the city of Alexandria, and I will come to you by the grace of God." He blessed me, and left me entranced.

The days I had waited in anticipation of this hour seemed forever. When the day had finally arrived, I doubled the blessing, as he requested, and waited for him outside the city. He approached me as if a thunderbolt or a mighty gust of wind which truly frightened me. I fell at his feet and kissed him, then gave him the blessings of flour and wine. He warmly said to me, "Do you long to see my fellow brethren?" to which I answered, "Yes master!" So he ordered, "Hold on to my vestment tightly and do not marvel over what you will see." The saint took hold of me and made the sign of the cross on my face saying, "Be strong!" After taking three steps, I was not aware of what was happening to me. I heard the sounds of mighty winds and crashing waves, and was incredibly frightened. Before dawn, we approached a great and beautiful monastery and entered its church. My eyes had never beheld such beauty. I followed this father into the church and saw a crowd of saintly fathers, and in fear of them, I trembled.

After celebrating the Holy Mass, and receiving the Holy Communion, I noticed a very old person who looked like a eunuch, standing at the door of the sanctuary and was supported on both sides by fellow fathers. The father who accompanied me said to the brethren, "Bless this priest who supplies us with the blessing of flour and wine each year!" So each one in turn put their hand on my head and blessed me. After this he said, "Now it is time for you to go back to

your home and church, because your people need you." I
implored him saying, "For the sake of God, please leave me
here with these saintly fathers!" But he answered, "This
is not possible...for whenever one of these fathers pass away,
the Lord replaces him..."[1]

I then asked, "Father, who is that elder who looks like
a eunuch and is supported by those two fathers?" He
answered, "Brother, this is the pure saint Annasimon, the
daughter of a king who inherited his kingdom, and left her
palace open for all, but she left everything, seeking our beloved
Lord Jesus Christ. There is no one here older than her, nor
higher in spirituality. She is our organiser and our spiritual
guardian who leads our thoughts in Christ Jesus through her
purity and holiness. She is the head over four hundred
fathers." I marvelled greatly and asked, "How do they
survive in the wilderness?" He answered, "Some eat from the
fruit of trees, others from the grass of the wilderness, and on
this day of Holy Thursday, every year, they come here and
gather together for Good Friday and Holy Saturday and
Easter Sunday, to celebrate and remember this special time
and partake of the Holy Body and Blood of our Lord Jesus
Christ. After taking each other's blessings, they return to
the wilderness and no one meets the other until Holy
Thursday the following year." He then turned to me and
said, "It is time for you to return to your town."

I left crying for departing this holy place, and as he farewelled
me, he said, "May Jesus Christ keep you!" I walked only a
short while and turned back but could not see the father or
the monastery. I became very thirsty and felt as if I was dying.
I dropped to the ground crying in desperation and suddenly I

---

[1] We have literally translated this paragraph from the Arabic text,
however, the Coptic Church does not believe that there is a 'fixed' number
of hermits.

found standing before me, that blessed father, so I rejoiced exceedingly. He took me by the hand and said, "Get up now and go home." As I began to walk, I heard mighty winds and crashing waves, and after a short time I found myself standing in front of my church door. I turned and found the father before me ordering, "Do not tell anyone of the things which have taken place until the day you die." He then blessed me and left. He continued visiting me each year to take the blessings of flour and wine, until the day my death approached.

These are the incidences I saw and witnessed with my own eyes regarding our holy desert fathers. Each time the blessed father would come to me, I would ask whether any of his fellow brethren had departed; in the hope of visiting them once more, but he would answer, "This is not possible..."

We ask our beloved Lord Jesus Christ, who glorifies and gives grace to His saints, to make us worthy of being together with them in His heavenly kingdom.

To our Lord be glory and honour forever, amen.

11. ABBA STRATIOS THE HERMIT

During the reign of one of the Orthodox kings over Rome, there lived a Roman prince who was responsible for one hundred soldiers. Filled with the grace of God, he expressed to the king his desire to leave this materialistic world and seek the company of God as a monk in the wilderness.

He sailed to Alexandria and then travelled on foot to Tor Sinai...This took place two hundred years after the death of Abba John Aklimakos, the writer of 'The Ladder of Virtues of the Sinai Fathers, and Abba Anastasi of Sinai, the guardian of monks'. During Abba John's time, there were two hundred and fifty monks residing in the Sinai monastery.

Abba Stratios dwelt in this monastery in strict ascetism; being fervent in spirit and in the love of our Lord Jesus Christ, and so he was clothed with the 'eskeem' of monasticism.

After spending several years living within the monastery and serving his fellow brothers with sincere love, he asked his spiritual father for his blessings and permission so that he may venture into the wilderness to dwell there.

He left, taking with him a head covering and a palm branch and went praising God saying, "I will lift up my eyes to the hills, from whence comes my help? My help comes from the Lord who made heaven and earth" (Psalm 121:1,2).

He kept walking until the Lord led him to a cave within the inner wilderness, and there he dwelt, in strict ascetism and fervencies and relentless spiritual struggle. He fed on the grass which grew on nearby rocks and drank fresh water from natural springs. He spent all his days praying and fasting, and only when he felt the need, would he feed upon a handful of grass and a mouthful of water. He lived as such for twelve years...

The Lord revealed to him that after forty days, he will depart from this temporary world and be united with the beloved Lord Jesus Christ, and the whole host of saints and angels. When Stratios felt the hour of his death approach, he made the sign of the cross in the wind and immediately the wind carried him and brought him safely inside the monastery. There he met his spiritual father who had aged very much, and when he saw Stratios, he asked, "Who are you?"

The saint replied, "I am your son Stratios, who resided with you in this monastery twelve years ago...I have come to you because my hour of deliverance is at hand, and I would like to spend the rest of my time on earth, here with my fathers in this monastery." His spiritual father embraced him with joy, then called all the monastery fathers to him, by ringing the bells. Immediately the fathers gathered and when they saw their fellow brother and hermit Stratios, they all rejoiced.

They gave him a separate cell, and after he entered, he closed the door...he then left the monastery without anyone seeing him, and went straight to the tomb of Abba John Aklimakos, the writer of the Sinai Fathers and Abba Anastasi. He knelt at Abba John's tomb so that the prayers of these blessed saints who lived two hundred years before him, may help him.

As he was kneeling and praying an angel of the Lord appeared to him and said, "Stratios, the two saints John and Anastasi have come to you to bless you, O pure saint, before you depart from this world." Stratios immediately turned and saw the two saints saying to him, "We will also be present during your deliverance and the release of your soul, and we will pray for you in the cell your fellow brothers have given you." Having said this, they departed and Stratios returned to his cell.

He did not tell anyone of the things which took place, except his disciple to whom he said, "My son, after thirty seven days pass, open the door of my cell, as it will be the day of my deliverance...do not be neglectful in this command, for I want you to bury my body..."

As the day approached, they knocked on his door, but no one answered. So they pushed open the door of his cell and found him kneeling and covered from head to toe in rough cloth...Beside him they found a censor filled with coal and burning of sweet smelling incense. This signified that the hermit fathers had come to pray on him...

The monastery fathers prayed on him, then buried him with great reverence and honour in the place where their saintly forefathers had been laid. From his pure body came the beautiful scent of incense, which was a blessing to many.

To our Lord be all glory, honour and worship now and unto the end of all ages, amen.

12. THE STORY OF A HERMIT FATHER

A Christian fisherman once said, "One day while I was fishing not far from the shores of Libya, I anchored the boat and ventured into the desert. As I roamed about looking for water, I found some wild plants and amidst them was a person. I asked, "Who are you?", and he answered, "I am a sailor, and was shipwrecked. I was saved by grabbing on to a drifting log which brought me safely to the shore. Travelling through the wilderness, I found these plants and this nearby spring of water, so I said to myself, 'Why should I return to the world after God has saved me from death and therefore wills that I live? It is better for me to remain with Christ here in this blessed place and leave the world with all its vain glories behind me.' I have chosen this path because of the infinite love of my Lord Jesus Christ, hoping that He may forgive me my countless sins. The Lord led me to a cave which belonged to the desert beasts. I entered and lived with them and we became friends, for they felt within me the life of repentance and the love of God. I eat from the grass and plants of the wilderness, and drink water from the spring..."

I asked him, "How long will you remain here?" and the saint answered, "On the same day next year, I ask you to bring some linen with which to wrap my body for burial." I kissed him and left, then headed back to Alexandria. Along the way, I made note of his residence so that the following year I would not lose direction.

After a year had passed, I packed some linen and went in search for this holy desert father. When we met, we embraced each other and he prayed for me. We then sat down and spoke about the many wonders and glories of our beloved Lord Jesus Christ.

I then lifted my head and looked at the saint and marvelled at the glorious light which shone from his face. The saint then did the sign of the cross saying, "Peace be to this blessed place and peace be to the world..." He then quietly released his soul.

Gently and carefully I wrapped the saint's body with complete respect; the beasts too revered the saint's body. I carried him to his cave and sealed the entrance with a large stone, then placed a wooden cross upon it.

I glorified the Lord and praised Him, then returned to Alexandria, speaking about the wonders of God and the sweet, aromatic life story of this blessed hermit father.

To our Lord be glory, honour and worship forever, amen.

13. ABBA MARCOS EL-TERMAKI THE HERMIT

Abba Serapion once said: I saw in a vision two hermits standing at the cave of Abba John the hermit. One of them said, 'Let us enter to take his blessings', but the other one answered him, 'Let us leave him to rest, for he must be tired from his journey in the wilderness.' As they spoke with each other, they mentioned how strange it was that Abba John had not yet seen Abba Marcos the elder of Mount Termaka; "for there is no other hermit or monk of his spiritually in the entire wilderness. Besides, Abba John has lived in the wilderness for many years and Abba Marcos being about one hundred and twenty years old had not yet seen the face of a fellow human for the past ninety five years...The Lord has revealed to Abba Marcos that after forty five days, he will depart this world to go to his Eternal Home...."

When I awoke I went to Abba John the hermit and told him all that I had seen in the vision, and said to him, "I know this mountain of Termaka, where the father resides!" After blessing me, I Serapion travelled to Alexandria, and arrived within five days; (usually a journey of twelve walking days), so I remembered the power of the vision I saw, and praised God...

Arriving in Alexandria, I asked a sailor for directions to Mount Termaka, and he responded, "It will take you twenty eight days to walk there, so I suggest you travel by sea, for it will be much easier than walking through the harsh wilderness."

Strengthening myself through the sign of the Cross, I took some dates and water and began my journey through valleys and deserts, and continued walking for ten days. During this time, I did not come across any human, animal or bird, because it was land where no rain fell, and no grass grew. After ten days of walking through the wilderness, I ran out of dates and water, and in exhaustion I collapsed to the ground. I had no strength to continue or to return, and suddenly as I lay helpless on the ground, I saw before me the two hermits I had seen in the vision. They approached me saying, "Why were you not patient to wait for us?" and when they noticed how tired I was, one of them said, "you need some water." He pulled out some green grass from the ground and gave it to me. Immediately after eating this, my strength was renewed by the grace of God, and I no longer felt hungry or thirsty. My heart was full of hope and courage, and so I got up and continued my journey until I sighted a cave. There I rested a while before continuing to walk another seven days. Finally I arrived at the foot of Mount Termaka, and prayed that God may give me the strength to climb to the top, so that I may receive the blessings of the saintly father. It took me three days to reach the top, and when I looked out from the heights of this mountain I found below me the terror and greatness of the ocean.

On the second night of being on this mountain, I saw angels crowding around the entrance of the saint's cave praising, "Blessed are you Abba Marcos; for the Lord has heard your prayers and has brought you Abba Serapion, for you have been anxious to see him!" I reverently approached the saint's cave and heard him saying, "How great are you O Lord for in your eyes one thousand years is like one day, so rejoice O my soul and do not fear the darkness!" He then came out of his cave and when he saw me he cried, "O my son you have arrived in peace; may God reward you according to your struggles. Come and greet your father!" As we embraced, he cried. I marvelled at his strength; for it was that of a youth.

He looked at me and said, "Brother Serapion, you are a spiritual monk, and beloved of God, and I was longing to see you for many years...May all glory be to our God who has enabled you to persist in your journey so that we might meet, for it has been ninety five years since I have seen a fellow human, or an animal, or even tasted bread. My son, I have spent thirty years of my ascetic life in several spiritual struggles. I hungered and I have thirsted; drinking only mouthfuls from the salty sea water. I was naked, and I suffered greatly from satanic wars. Many times devils would throw me from the top of this mountain, until no flesh remained on my bones, nor hair on my skin, and they would scream at me in the darkness of the night, "Get out of our land!" But despite all of this, I remained patient; withstanding hunger, thirst, and nakedness.

Then God in His mercy and love, allowed the hair on my skin to grow so that it may protect my body, and cover it from nakedness, and daily He sent me food and angels to minister unto me. My beloved Serapion, I have seen Paradise, and the glory which God has prepared for those who love Him. I have seen Enoch, Elijah, and all the righteous fathers, I have also seen Abba Anthony the Great, the father of all the monks standing in great glory! God has revealed to me many wonders, and whatever I have asked for in His name, He has granted me."

I then asked him, "My holy father Marcos, for the love of God, please tell me for what reason you have come to this place?" He warmly smiled at me saying, "My dear son I was brought up in the town of Atnas, and was a student of Arts and Philosophy. When my father died, I thought to myself, 'I too shall die like my father and leave this world, but by my own free will, before my Lord forces it upon me.' I got up and sailed by sea, asking the Lord to save my soul and guide my way...The waves carried me along and eventually directed me to this mountain..."

When morning dawned, I looked at the body of Abba Marcos and found it to be just skin on bones, and I became frightened, but his gentle heartfelt my apprehension , and so he turned to me and said, "Do not be afraid of my weary appearance. Now tell me, how is the world?" I answered,

"Father, the world today is much better than it was in the past; Christianity is shining forth like a brilliant sun, and the worship of idols has ceased..." The saintly father rejoiced exceedingly and gave thanks to God. He then asked, "Are there any people in the world who do wonders in the name of our Lord; for He has taught us, 'If you have faith as a mustard seed, you shall say to this mountain move from here to there, and it will move and nothing will be impossible for you' (Matthew 17:20)." Having said this, immediately the mountain trembled, but the saint because of his tremendous faith, struck the mountain and at once, it quietened. As for me the weak Serapion, I feared greatly but the saint encouraged me saying, " My son Serapion, do not wonder about the power and the greatness of God," and then he continued, "Blessed is the Lord God almighty, who led me to this blessed place! Let us stand and pray." He outstretched his hands towards the heavens, and prayed Psalm 23.

After praying, he turned towards the cave's entrance and said, "Prepare something for us to eat," then turning to me he said, "The Lord will provide for us from the abundance of His mercy." I became very confused, for I could not see who he was talking to. It only occurred to me later that he was talking to the angels.

When we entered the cave, we found a beautiful table and upon it white bread, delicious fruit, two pieces of fish, olives and a jug of water. Abba Marcos then asked me, "Abba Serapion, please bless the food!", but I answered, "Forgive me my father." He then lifted his eyes towards heaven, blessed the food and made the sign of the cross. While we were eating, Abba Marcos said to me, "Abba Serapion, everyday my Lord provides for me one piece of fish, but today because of His goodness, He has provided for us two!" We ate from the table, prepared for us by the Lord's angels, and then praised our beloved Jesus for His many gifts which He grants for those who love Him. I had never tasted such delicious food, nor drank sweeter water! Abba Marcos said, "This has been my food for the past sixty years. I have suffered greatly from satanic wars, and many times I would cry and be afraid, but the Lord sustained me. After thirty five years of relentless spiritual struggle, the Lord was merciful and enabled the hair on my skin to grow and cover me. No longer could the devils approach me, and no longer did I hunger or thirst or become ill.

My days on earth are now completed, and the time for my departure from this world is quickly approaching." Having said this, we got up to pray and we began with the Psalms of David...

"Abba Serapion, follow me and come to the cave where I used to reside, for I would like you to bury my body within it." When we entered the cave, a light shone brightly like the rays of a sun, and I smelt the sweet aroma of incense. My saintly father Abba Marcos farewelled the cave saying, "Peace be to you O holy, blessed cave, for you have sheltered my poor body, and within you I shall rest until the Day of Judgement and the resurrection of my body, when the Lord will raise it up to eternity!" Then I followed him to the top of the mountain, and he said, "Peace be to the entire world, and to all the churches of my Lord, and peace be to His blessed flock; may He preserve you all by His grace!" Then he turned to me and through gentle eyes, said, "Abba Serapion, stay with me just for this night, and keep watch with me, for on this night my soul shall be released from my weak body, and I ask you for the sake of our beloved Lord, do not even take one hair from my body. Do not wrap my body in anything, but just place it as it is in the cave which I have shown you, then seal its entrance with a stone, and the right hand of God shall protect it!"

When I heard these words, I fell at his feet crying bitterly and begged him saying, "My blessed father, take me to the place where you are going!" But he answered me lovingly, "The

Lord is the only One who knows the place to where I am going." As he was saying this, I heard a great and fearful voice from heaven declaring, "Bring to Me the good and righteous servant, who has been doing the will of My father; come Marcos and rest in the place of Eternal peace!" I feared this voice exceedingly...Then I heard this same voice once again: "Stretch out your hands and complete your struggle!" Immediately I saw two angels carrying bright garments with which they carried the pure soul of the saint up to heaven. I then heard an angel exclaiming to an army of devils, "Depart and disperse from the light you soldiers of darkness and evil!" I gazed at the soul of the saint which was ascending higher and higher, and I heard again the voice exclaiming, "Depart you soldiers of darkness from this righteous soul!"

As the soul of the blessed saintly father continued to ascend, I saw a hand of fire stretched out to receive the soul, and then I saw them no more...I began praying on the pure saint, and after I had finished, I carried his body with complete respect, and carefully lay him within his cave just as he had requested, and then sealed its entrance with a large stone. Descending from the mountain, I wept bitterly...through my tears I sighted the two hermits whom I had seen in a vision, approaching me: "Peace be to you Serapion, for you have been blessed by Abba Marcos the hermit, whom the whole world is not worthy of!" As we walked together, I fell into a deep sleep, and when I awoke I found myself at the entrance of Abba John's cave. Abba John came out and blessed me, and when we sat together, I told him of all that I had seen of the blessed saint of God - Marcos the hermit, and of the two hermits who accompanied me.

He answered me saying, "Truly father, we are not worthy to be considered monks, for we have never experienced any struggle in comparison to the relentless struggles of the virtuous saint Marcos, but let us ask and implore our Lord, through the pleadings of Abba Anthony, the father of all monks, and through the pleadings of Abba Marcos who is blessed amongst all the saints, and all the righteous fathers, to grant us His mercy and to forgive us our sins, so that we may partake of the inheritance of His Kingdom with the rest of His saints.

To our Lord be honour, worship, and glory forever more, Amen.

14. THE HERMIT

Some of the hermit fathers approached Abba John el Tabaisi in Mount Assuit to ask him about the lives and virtues of the desert fathers, and of the spiritual visions which are revealed to them. Abba John said to them, "In the first place, you must be humble, denying all worldly and bodily cares, and you must be in deep love with our Lord Jesus Christ. Those who do not possess these virtues shall be like leaves that fall from the tree and die."

It was Abba John's practice to speak to people on Sundays through a small hole in his cave, and so likewise he spoke with the hermit fathers. He continued: "In the monastery situated in the valley of Mount Assuit, resided one of my spiritual sons. One day he came to me asking for my blessings so that he could venture into the inner wilderness and live there as an ascetic; he was still a youth at the time. He walked for many days in the wilderness until he came to a place where no animal, nor human nor plant has ever been. He found for himself a small, dark cave, and there he dwelt.

On the first day, he went searching for food and water, but found none. On the second day an angel of the Lord appeared to him carrying bread and water for the young ascetic. He blessed him saying, "I shall bring for you bread and water every second day, so do not waste your time and efforts in searching for food." The angel granted him peace, then departed. For thirty years the angel provided for him bread and water, and he regularly partook of Holy Communion in churches, without anyone seeing him; just like our blessed hermit fathers.

One wintery day, he sat at the entrance of his cave and gazed at the beauty of the dew drops glistening in the rising sun. So instead of glorifying God for His wonderful creation, he said to himself, "The Lord has formed these beautiful crystals because of my prayers", and he began to be very proud in his thoughts.

As the evil one started to sow the seeds of ungodly intentions in his mind. He continued tempting him by means of reminding him of his life before monasticism - his freedom, his friends, and the delicious food he used to eat and enjoy. Immediately the saint began complaining about the simplicity of the food which the angel provided for him, and greatly desired to have abundance of food; just as the Israelites complained to Moses and Aaron in the midst of the wilderness. The saint even cried for being cut off from all worldly pleasures.

Two days had passed since the time he noticed the dewdrops. This time the angel did not appear to him, but left his food outside the cave. When the saint went searching for his food, he found the bread mouldy, yet because of his hunger he ate it and drank the water provided for him. This was his first punishment for leaving the Lord's embrace to listen to the voice of Satan; but ignoring this warning, he chose not to repent. He persisted in his unrighteous thoughts to the extent that he listened to the evil one's voice when he was reminding the saint of the Old Testament prophets who married, like Abraham, Issac and Jacob...and so our saint in his wandering thoughts forgot that he was consecrated to the Lord...

This time, the bread the angels brought to him was not only mouldy but bitter, (symbolising the bitterness of sin). When the saint refused to adhere to the warnings to repent, he heard the voice of an angel angrily saying to him, "Poor man, depart from this place because you are not worthy to live here...!" So he took his rod and returned to the monastery of Abba John el Tabaisi, where he began his consecrated life as a monk."

He approached the cell of his spiritual father Abba John who was then ninety years old. The spiritual elder opened the shutter of the cave's hole and saw a man standing before him crying bitterly. Abba John not recognising him asked, "Who are you?" to which the saint replied, "I am your son the hermit, who has dwelt in the wilderness for the past thirty years, but because of my numerous sins, I heard a voice ordering me to, "...go back to the monastery and repent before all the brethren, for you are no longer worthy to remain in this place!"

Abba John accepted his repentance and encouraged him by saying, "Our beloved Lord Jesus Christ is a merciful God who came to save sinners and to carry the lost sheep on His shoulders. Now, go into the monastery and work in the mill with the animals, so that you may remember the repentance of Samson, and remember the humility of our Lord who was born in a stable, and remember how Satan fell from the heights of heaven like lightening because of his pride. Although you have glorified yourself instead of glorifying God, the Lord has said that no matter how much a person sins, God will forgive them through repentance: '...though your sins are like scarlet, they shall be as white as snow; though they are red like crimson, they shall be as white as wool' (Isaiah 1:18)."

When his fellow brothers saw him, they rejoiced at his return. They washed his feet and dressed him in new cloth, for he was near naked, and continually they supported and encouraged him through their words of spiritual benefit.

The saint worked in the mill doing the work of the animals, as his spiritual father had advised, for the rest of his days on earth. He ate his bread crying bitterly for his past sins and repented daily.

A year had passed since he returned to the monastery, and he died in peace. The monastery fathers buried him with great honour, while giving praise and thanks to our merciful God.

To whom is due all glory forever, amen.

15. ABBA ELIJAH THE HERMIT

Abba Elijah was one of the fathers from Tor-Sinai, and one of the spiritual sons of Abba Silwanis of Mount Sinai. He lived his life in ascetic order, just like Elijah the prophet. The cave in which he resided was several kilometres away from the monastery, and there he practised diligently praying and fasting, and was a true example of holiness and righteousness. He dwelt in his cave for fifty one years, during which time he increased daily in spirituality and he never delayed in partaking of the Holy Communion and attending the Holy Masses in the monastery without being seen.

One night, a brother from the monastery came to the saint to seek his blessings and ask him about his spiritual life. As he approached the saint's cave, he noticed strong rays of bright light shining forth from the cave's window. He was astonished and stood entranced over this sight for three hours. When the saint had completed his prayers, a pillar of light which stretched from his cave to the heavens, slowly faded. The monk knocked on the saint's door, and when the saint came out, he could not bear to look at the saint's face because of the brilliant light which shone forth from him like the rays of a sun. The saint knew by the Spirit that this brother had seen the rays of light and the pillar of light which shone brightly during his prayers, and when he asked, "My son, have you seen anything unusual?" he answered, "Glory be to our Lord Jesus Christ who glorifies His saints!", so the saint realised that it was God's will that this vision be revealed to the brother.

As they sat together, the saint spoke words of spiritual wisdom and then turned to his new disciple, the brother, saying, "My son, I have avoided keeping company with fellow humans because I do not deserve their praise and honour; only God, glory be to Him, deserves all praise and honour. As for us mere men, we are weak and sinners, but do not dismay, for I shall pray with you in the monastery, however, some will see me and others won't..."

They embraced each other and then the disciple left, venturing into the wilderness until he came to a cave. He spent the next seven years praying without ceasing, and fed on the grass of the wilderness.

Seven years later, the saint visited his disciple's cave and knocked on its door. When the disciple saw him, he was greatly surprised and so he did the sign of the cross. The saint said to him, "Well done my son, for even demons appear in the form of saints!...I am Elijah your father." The disciple fell down and cried for he had not seen Abba Elijah for many years. The saint comforted him and said, "My dear son, did I not tell you that I do not prefer keeping company with other humans? I have been dwelling in my distant cave and attending the Holy Mass regularly in the monastery, but not everyone could see me." The disciple exclaimed, "But father, I never saw you!" to which the saint replied, "It was not God's will, but I have come to you now because it is time for me to leave this world and dwell in the place of Eternal living. So I ask you to please pray on me, and place my body in the cave where I lived my life in ascetism." Having said this, he embraced his disciple, prayed for a short while before stretching his body and delivering his soul. His disciple cried bitterly for many days, and finally he went to the abbot of the monastery to tell him about the saint and his blessed departure. The abbot at once gathered the monastery fathers together and went to the cave of this righteous man. The fathers prayed on him and then buried him with great honour and respect, giving thanks and praise to God who glorifies His saints.

To Him is due all glory, honour and worship now and forever more, amen.

16. OUR BLESSED HERMIT FATHER

St. John Chrysostom once said: One day, I thought of visiting those who lived on the islands of the Mediterranean, for they are within my Diocese. Journeying by boat, I took with me deacons and priests and sailed to the island of Cyprus.

There we identified human footprints, but could not see anyone. As we followed the footprints in the sand, we came to a place which resembled a church built of uncarved rocks, and between the rocks was coral. There was no door and no windows. We entered and found light shining strongly from seven fathers who stood praying, like seven bright stars. We remained in our positions praying with them, and when they had finished, they turned towards us and prostrated before me, and then greeted us. I John, said to them, "I am John, your father and patriarch." Again they prostrated before me, and said to my weakness, "Our beloved Lord Jesus Christ has brought you here to bless us and to encourage us by seeing you." I said to them, "Please, tell me your story..."

"A long time ago, the seven of us gathered together from Constantinople and journeyed to this island to spend our lives in worship and in the peace of our Lord Jesus Christ. On the day of our arrival, we collected rocks to build caves so that we may be sheltered from the rough winds of the sea, and on the second day we began building this church.

We eat from the weeds that grow between the rocks and drink from the sea. As for all these sand dunes which surround the church, we have been wanting to remove them, however, we cannot find the time, for our minds and thoughts are constantly engaged with our Lord Jesus Christ."

I asked him, "Where is your spiritual father?" and as soon as I had asked this, an old man approached me leaning on a rod saying, "I am your servant." Noticing that he was near naked, I asked, "Do you require some cloth to cover your body?" He answered, "The Lord protects and shields us from the coldness of winter and the heat of summer." I asked, "Do you need any food?" to which he replied, "We feed on these weeds which are sufficient for us, and therefore we are not in need of anything from the world." I then said, "Father, please pray for me and for the safety of the church."

After taking the blessings of these holy hermit fathers, we left glorifying the name of our beloved Lord Jesus Christ;

to whom is due all glory and honour forever, amen.

17. ABBA HERMINA THE HERMIT

The blessed saint Abahor el Abarhati records for us the story of the most excellent saint Abba Hermina the hermit, of Mount Kaw:

"I was living with Abba John and Abba Yousab on Mount Asfaht, when one day as we were walking through the wilderness, clothed in weaved palm, we noticed a person who resembled a spirit, and his face shone with light as bright as the sun. He approached and bowed before us saying, "Do not be afraid, for I am John the Evangelist and beloved disciple of our eternal God and Lord Jesus Christ. Hasten Abahor and journey into the inner wilderness for there you will find a righteous man by the name of Hermina, and you shall know him for he wears a 'kolonsowa' upon his head (the monk's head covering). He is from the region of El Bahnasa and he has lived in the wilderness for the past sixty years in relentless spiritual struggle."

Anxiously I asked St John about Abba Hermina's life. "From the age of ten, he shepherded his father's cattle and diligently learnt all the psalms and how to pray. He fasted everyday without food until the evening, except for Saturday and Sunday. He had great love for all people and was modest in all things. If a stranger would pass him by, he would joyfully welcome him saying, "Please come and grace me with your presence by sharing a meal with me at my home." He served them with precious Christian love, giving them water to drink from the well, carrying their luggage and walking a mile with them, before returning happily to his flock.

In his virtues, he reached perfection, and so one day St. Peter and I disguised ourselves as monks passing in his direction. He was in the field shepherding his cattle and when he saw us, he came forth and warmly welcomed us. He asked us to rest in his village until the morning, but we declined saying, "It is better for us to go to the monastery and rest with our brothers the monks." He then requested, "Please, take me with you because in the Holy Bible it says, 'There is no one who has left home or brothers or sisters or father or mother or wife or children or lands for my sake and the gospel's who shall not receive one hundred fold now in this time' (Mark 10:29,30)." I asked him if he was willing to become a monk, and eagerly he replied, "I am ready if my Lord is willing, and through your prayers."

At once I took a pair of scissors and cut his hair then dressed him in the holy, angelic 'eskeem' of monasticism. We lead him to the monastery where he received the Holy Communion and then we prayed for him that our beloved Lord Jesus Christ may bless him and save him from the traps of the enemy, so that the name of God will be glorified through him in every place he goes.

We left him in the care of Abba Jacob the abbot so that he may teach him about the rites of monasticism, before the Lord Jesus leads him to the place He has chosen for him.

From the moment Hermina entered the monastery, Abba Jacob was very happy with him, and when the time had come in which God arranged for him to leave the monastery, I John knocked on his door and entered his cell. He prostrated before me (which is a common monastic habit), and together we prayed.

After praying I said, "Let us go to the southern region of Mount Kaw, for it is called the mountain of joy and consolation." Before leaving the monastery, Abba Hermina went to Abba Jacob and prostrated before him saying, "Forgive me my father and pray for me, for I am going to Mount Kaw in Upper Egypt in order to have the blessings of all the saints, and may your blessings also be with me." So Abba Jacob blessed him, and then together we departed.

On our journey, we met an elder named Bishoy who said, "Rest here until the morning, then continue in God's peace." In the morning we continued walking southward and as the sun set, we found a cloud of light before us, so Hermina turned to me and said, "Master, as yet I do not know your name." So I turned to him and said, "I am John, the son of Zebedee, and at the time in which we clothed you in the holy 'eskeem' of monasticism, the apostles Peter and Paul and David the King were present with me..."

We arrived at Mount Elnakloon, which is known as the Mountain of Rock, and we heard the sounds of hymns and praises; as it was the ninth hour on Saturday evening. We listened and joined in the praises until the dawn of Sunday morning. The place where we stood praying was the area in which the grave of Abba Elijah was.

We continued journeying south until we came to the foot of Mount Assuit, and then further walked for another two days through a very deep valley. We sighted a cave which was located in a high position, and directly below it ran a stream of fresh spring water surrounded by beautiful palm trees bearing fruit. I John turned to Hermina and said, "Live here in this blessed place, eating from the fruits of these trees and drinking from this spring..." I blessed him, then departed.

Abba Hermina began his new ascetic life in relentless spiritual struggle. He prayed fervently and fasted diligently, and daily he prostrated two thousand four hundred times - one thousand two hundred prostrations during his morning prayers and one thousand two hundred prostrations at night. Angels would constantly come to comfort him and strengthened him in his spiritual life, including Archangel Michael who is the helper of saints dwelling in the wilderness for the sake of the Lord.

Abba Hermina continued to live for many years in

strict ascetism, until his eyes were deeply set in his face, and his body became weak. Many times the Lord revealed to him the place prepared for the righteous saints and those who love God, and many times he was caught up into the third heaven; just like the Apostle Paul.

The devil was furious and greatly envied the many crowns prepared for Abba Hermina. So one day the devil disguised himself as an angel and went to the saint saying, "Hermina, get up for you must go back to the monastery and live with Abba Jacob!", but the saint knew by the Spirit that this apparition is not from God and so he said, "Who are you?" to which the devil replied "I am Michael who stands in the presence of God!" So the saint replied, "If it is so, let us stand to pray before we begin our journey." But the devil answered, "No, for I cannot pray without my host of angels!" The saint then said, "In the name of my Lord Jesus Christ, I tell you I shall not leave this place until you reveal to me who you are!" And having said this, Abba Hermina began to pray. Immediately a cloud of fire descended from heaven in order to consume the devil. Burning, he screamed out to Abba Hermina to save him from the fire, so the saint because of his great Christian love, released him. The devil turned to the saint and said, "I will not rest until I defeat you and all those like you!" and with this he disappeared.

Satan could no longer tolerate the saint's strong spirituality, so he gathered together an army of his soldiers and said, "Let us go and conquer Hermina, for he disobeys my voice and my will! We must overcome him with our power and rob him of his glory!" The angel of the Lord appeared to the saint and said, "Blessed Hermina, be strong and let not your heart tremble in fear, for the Lord is with you."

The devil disguised himself as a glorious king, accompanied by seventy of his soldiers. They approached the saint's cave and knocked on his door. Hermina came out praying the psalms of David and when he saw them, he made the sign of the cross saying, "The Lord sends me help from heaven..." Then the Archangels Michael and Gabriel descended from the heights and scourged the soldiers until they screamed out, "Have mercy, for we have been ordered by our chief to destroy Hermina, so release us and we shall never return to this place again!" When Satan who was disguised as a king saw this, he became like the wind and vanished with his soldiers far into the wilderness. The saint rejoiced saying, "I was tempted to fall, but the Lord sustained me; for He is my holy and blessed salvation. That is why my lips shall sing forth Your praise, and Your name shall be glorified forever!"

The devil kept watch from a distance and finally sent one of his evil soldiers, who returned to the saint as a mighty sandstorm which completely covered and buried his cave. The saint then lifted up his eyes towards heaven and prayed, "O merciful and beloved Lord who heard the prayers of the three youth from the fiery furnace and saved them, and heard the prayer of Daniel from the lions' den and saved him, and heard the prayer of father Abraham and listened to Susanna and saved her. You heard the prayer of Joseph from the torment of prison and saved him, please, I ask You to hear me now and send to me Your angel..!" At once the Archangel Michael appeared, chained the devil and said to Abba Hermina, "The Lord Jesus Christ has placed the devil in your hands, so that you may do with him what you will." Having said this, he ascended to the heavens.

The saint then turned to the devil and said, "O you enemy who battles with the godly, I tell you that by the living God, I shall not release you before you have removed all the sand that surrounds my cave." At once the devil became like a lion and began shovelling the sand until it was completely removed. Again the saint said to the devil, "I will not release you until I torment you like you torment the saints!" The devil then screamed out to his leader, "Did we not tell you to leave Hermina, the man of God in peace, lest he does to us what was done by Abba Bebnoda, who ordered a large rock to crush you on Mt Tookh?!" The devil begged and screamed to the saint for mercy and promised that if he is released he will never return, so the saint glorified God saying, "Heaven and Earth and all that is in them praise You, for by Your breath they were created and because of Your great love, You do not allow our enemies to trample over us. To You is all glory and power forever, amen!"

After this incidence, the blessed saint Hermina ventured to the south of Kaw. As he crossed the river, he heard voices coming from the bodies of saints saying, "Blessed is your presence with us today our beloved brother Hermina!" Together they glorified God who is the only performer of miracles. He remained there praying unceasingly throughout the days and nights, and at sunset he would eat only a little of the fruits which fell from the trees, for they tasted as sweet as honey in his mouth, and he drank from fresh spring water. In everything, he crossed himself and gave thanks to God...and when the forty days of the Great Fast were finished, the Lord gave him new strength."

I John the Beloved then turned to Abahor and said, "Now I have told you the story of the blessed man of God Hermina, so arise now and search for him for he is well advanced in years, and his body has become weak from his strict ascetic life. You shall find him dwelling in a cave in Mount Kaw. Record his story as I have told it to you, for it will become a great consolation to its reader."

After St. John blessed me, I Abahor immediately got up in search of this blessed man of God Hermina. I walked within the depths of the wilderness and eventually journeyed into a deep valley and there before my eyes was the blessed Hermina, standing before a well with his hands outstretched in prayer. From his hands came forth beams of light which reached up to the heights of heaven, and a cloud of sweet smelling incense surrounded him. I carefully approached and knelt before him. He prayed for me then said, "Blessed is your coming to me today Abahor el Kesar, for the Lord has sent you to me." When we sat down together, I asked him to tell me about his life, and he responded with the same words of St John the Beloved...

I remained with him for two days before returning to my place, but after some time had passed, I got up and once again journeyed in search of the blessed man of God. Along the way, I fell into a deep sleep and I dreamt of a host of angels dressing Hermina in garments of light while honouring and blessing him. When I awoke from this beautiful dream, I anxiously continued my journey until I reached the saint's cave.

When Abba Hermina saw me, he rejoiced in the Spirit and his face shone as bright as the sun. I prostrated before him and then we embraced one another. We spoke about the many wonders of God and later Abba Hermina said to me, "Brother Abahor, let us continue in our spiritual struggle for a while longer, for the traps of the devil are many, and let us always bear in our mind and heart that we are strangers in this world, and we must weep for our many sins." After being filled with Abba Hermina's grace and spiritual words, I returned joyfully to my cave in Mount Akhmeem.

Six months later, St John the Beloved of the Lord Jesus Christ came to my cave clothed in light, so immediately I fell at his feet. He blessed me and raised me up saying, "Go now to your friend Hermina because the day of his departure quickly approaches, for it is time for him to rest from the hardships of this world." Having said this, he left. I stood to pray, and in the afternoon I ventured into the wilderness of Kaw. Along the way, I confronted a large, black ox with two horns. I advanced towards it while doing the sign of the cross and immediately it vanished in the wind. I then glorified the Lord who saved me from the evil one.

I continued walking within the wilderness until I found Hermina kneeling on the ground praying. He had remained as such for forty days in fervent prayer. When I saw this sight, I wept bitterly for my weakness and my struggles which are in no way comparable to the beloved saint's. I then looked up and behold, I saw the Lord Jesus Christ, glory be to Him, descend from heaven upon the chariot of the Cherubim amidst a whole host of angels praising, and He spoke to Abba Hermina saying, "Blessed are you My chosen one, for you shall be rewarded many fold. I will make your name known in the entire world and I have prepared for you three glorious crowns : one for your chastity, one for your living as a stranger in this world, and one for the many hardships which you have endured for the sake of My name. Now, go to the north of this mountain so that you may be blessed by the bodies of the saints which are present there, then return here to the south of Kaw to dwell for the remainder of your life. When you return to this place, you shall live for a further six months before completing your journey on earth, which will be on the second of Kiakh; and indeed your friend Abahor shall also depart on the same day a year later. Both your soul and Abahor's shall be with Me in the place of Eternal Living, but for now, Abahor will take care of your body along with Abba Yousab!" The Lord then blessed him, bestowed His peace upon him, and then ascended in great glory.

After this glorious revelation, Abba Hermina clothed himself in the monastic habit and on top of his 'tonya' (tunic) he wore a tunic of weaved palm leaves. Together we crossed the river and headed westward. Along the way we met Abba Armia who greeted us saying, "Welcome my beloved brother Hermina whom God has granted to the city of Kaw and all its surrounding regions!" We then ascended northward where we were carried up in a cloud and taken to the church of Abba Elijah; the church where his body is laid. Later, we walked to the church of Abba Apollo to receive the blessings of his pure body and pray in his church.

We then met Abba Jacob who was reading spiritual stories to his brethren, and in his church we received the Holy Communion.

From there we headed towards the north of El Khataf where we found the blessed body of Abba Mina. We kissed his pure body before returning southward to the mountain of Abba Abanoub the Confessor, and from his body we heard a voice saying, "Blessed is your coming to us today Abba Hermina...for the mention of your name is like sweet smelling fragrance in the city of Kaw and all over the world!" Following this, the Archangel Michael appeared to Abba Hermina saying, "I am Michael who cares for all the Lord's saints; prepare yourself for after twelve days you will be released from this world."

On the first of Kiakh, I Abahor came out of my cell, and together with my fellow brethren, we went to Abba Hermina. At our arrival we embraced each other and he kissed me saying, "Brother, please remember me, for my hour approaches in which my soul shall be released from my body...I ask you to wrap my body and lay it in the place which my Lord Jesus Christ has prepared for me until the day of the Resurrection of the bodies...O Abahor, how fearful it is for me to stand between the hands of the living God and the hour of death. Are you too father afraid of that hour?" So I Abahor answered him, "Which human on earth could not fear such an hour? But blessed is the man whose fear is in the Lord and who abides in His love and commandments." An angel of the Lord then appeared before us and said to Abba Hermina, "Your friends Abahor and Yousab the hermits, will take care of your body..." The saint rejoiced exceedingly at these words.

I looked at my saintly father Hermina and found that his face became full of light, so I began to cry. When he felt this, he turned to me and said warmly, "Why are you crying?" to which I answered, "Because you will go and leave me!" He looked at me with gentle eyes and said, "My dear brother Abahor, as the name of Elijah is known throughout all the lands, so too will your name be, and it will be a blessing for all, and the Lord will perform many miracles in your name." Having said these words, he then embraced me and returned to his cell.

On the second day of the blessed Coptic month Kiakh, my saintly father Hermina died, and with my own eyes I witnessed the heavenly hosts embrace the saint's soul in a garment of light and carry him towards heaven in a glorious chariot. The Archangels Michael and Gabriel were present, and the whole angelic host were heard singing songs of praise and sounding their trumpets all the way to the Heavenly Jerusalem. I stood to pray before wrapping the body of the pure and beloved saint and taking its blessings. I then told my fellow brethren all that I had seen."

From this time on, Abba Hermina had become the patron saint of Kaw and all the surrounding regions. He appeared many times and performed many miracles. His body still remains in the monastery of Abba Hermina, which is located to the north of Kaw, towards Badari in the province of Assuit. In the twelfth century, a church was built in his name in the city of Homilis (El Bahnassa); the town in which he was brought up.

May his blessings and prayers be with us all and all glory be to God forever, amen.

18. THE HERMIT FATHERS

After burying the pure body of Abba Noufer the hermit, Abba Bebnoda met with other desert fathers and said: After I buried Abba Noufer's body, I walked in the wilderness for four days and nights, after which time I noticed a cave. I approached it and knocked on its door, but no one answered. After sitting at its entrance for about an hour, I thought to myself, 'perhaps the father who lives in this cave has passed away!'

At once, the saintly looking father came out of his cave, as though the Spirit had revealed to him my thoughts. He was of fine appearance. He had a long white beard and was clothed in weaved palm leaves. When he saw me he said, "You are brother Bebnoda who had buried the body of the blessed saint Abba Noufer." Immediately I fell at his feet, but he raised me up saying, "Get up my beloved brother, for it is the Lord who has revealed this to me, and He has told me to await your coming to me today. It has been sixty years since I have seen anyone, besides my fellow desert fathers who also reside on this mountain."

While he was speaking with me, three more hermit fathers approached me saying, "You are our beloved brother Bebnoda, and our fellow friend in Christian deeds. Our blessed Lord has revealed to us of your coming today, for the four of us have spent sixty years on this mountain without seeing anyone else." I then saw before me five loaves of bread which looked as if they had been freshly baked. We got up to pray before eating the loaves together. The fathers said to me, "All these years the Lord has provided for us daily four loaves, but because of your presence with us today, the Lord has sent us five."

After eating we stood to pray. It was a Sunday night and we remained praying until the morning. I asked if I could spend the rest of my life with them, but they answered, "This is not the will of God, but rather, go into the land of Egypt and tell all people about the things which you have seen!" I asked them to tell me their names, but they replied, "It is only for us to know each other's names, but we ask you to remember us brother, until we meet in the Kingdom of Heaven, and take care that you not be overcome by the world."

After praying for me, they blessed me and foretold me of the things which will take place on my journey back to Egypt. I walked for several days before seeing a spring of water and palm trees surrounding it, so I sat within their shade and meditated on the many wonders of God. I wondered about the beautiful fragrant palm trees which grew in the midst of the wilderness and the sweet tasting fruits which they bear. I also wondered about the fresh spring of water which overflowed in abundance, to quench anyone's thirst. I then said to myself, "Indeed, this is God's paradise!"

While I was sitting within the shade of the trees, I saw from afar four men dressed in sheepskin walking in my direction. "You are our beloved Bebnoda" they said, and at once I fell at their feet. After we greeted one another, we prayed, then spoke about the many glories of our Beloved Lord Jesus Christ. My heart rejoiced exceedingly in their presence.

I asked them, "My dear brothers, from where have you come, and who has lead you to this place?" They replied, "We are from the town of El Bahnassa. When we had finished our education, we said to one another, 'We have learnt all the wisdom of this passing world, and now we must also learn the wisdom of the eternal world.' We considered this thought daily until we decided that the best way to learn about the wisdom of God is to dedicate our entire life and time to Him. For this reason we ventured into the wilderness...

We took with us bread and water, and after many days of walking in the wilderness, we saw a person full of light standing before us. He held our hands and lead us to this place, and we have been drinking from this fresh spring and feeding from the fruits of these trees ever since. On our arrival, we found a saintly old father, whom the angel commanded to teach us the life of worship and spiritual contemplation, so we remained with him a whole year. After the year had passed, our blessed father passed away to the Kingdom of God, and now we remain alone in this place. At the end of each week, we meet here in order that we may pray together."

I Bebnoda remained with them for seven days, during which time I asked for their names. The first father replied, "My name is John" and the second responded with, "Andrew", but the remaining two preferred not to tell me their names. After blessing me they said that it was time for me to return to my monastery, so they walked with me the first six miles, then departed. I continued my journey through the wilderness for several days, crying, for my heart was deeply saddened for having left them.

Eventually I arrived at my monastery and told my fellow brethren in Christ all that I had seen and heard of the pure saint Abba Noufer the hermit, and all the blessed hermit fathers whom I had met and spoken with. May the blessings of their prayers be with us,

to our Lord Jesus Christ be all glory, honour and dominion forever, amen.

19. ABBA PAULA, THE FIRST HERMIT

Born in the province of Tiba (Luxor, Upper Egypt) in the year 229 A.D., Paula was the second son of a very rich man. When the father died, the two sons wanted to share the inheritance, so Peter, being the eldest, took the majority and gave what was left over to his brother Paula. This action caused great friction between the two brothers, and because they could not come to an agreement, they decided to settle the matter in court.

Along the way, they noticed a coffin being carried, and a great multitude mourning the loss. Paula approached one of the men to find out who had died, and the man responded, "Son, this man who died today, delighted in luxuries and lived the life of indulgence, possessed large amounts of gold and silver, and always dressed in expensive attire. Today he left the world and all his riches behind. Take heed my son that we not follow his example, but rather persist in enduring spiritual struggles, for blessed is the man who lives in this world, but does not belong to this world, for the Lord will reward him richly in His Heavenly Kingdom."

Paula heard these words and felt as if he was spiritually awakened, and suddenly the world before him seemed as nought. He turned to his brother and said, "Brother, let us return." As they were returning home, Paula walked slowly behind his brother, then quickly escaped from his sight. Peter searched for days, and when he could not find his brother, he cried bitterly, "Why did I quarrel with my brother on worldly riches?!"

Having left the town, Paula found an empty tomb, and so he remained within it for three days and three nights, in continuous meditation and prayer. On the fourth day, an angel of the Lord appeared to him and led him into the inner Eastern Wilderness. The angel directed him into a deserted cave, which was located near a spring of water and a fruitful palm tree. He dressed himself in a tunic he weaved from palms, and diligently prayed,

"My Lord Jesus Christ, Son of the living God, save me from the traps of the enemy, be merciful to me so that I may accomplish Your will and rest safely between Your hands, for to You my King, is all glory and power forever, amen!"

He began his ascetic life in the Eastern Wilderness in the year 250 A.D., and remained there for 80 years.

Abba Anthony meets Abba Paula:

One day, Abba Anthony thought to himself proudly, "I am the first person to ever venture into and live in the inner wilderness!" but the Lord revealed to him that, "within this wilderness lives a person whom the whole world is not worthy of his footstep." Immediately Abba Anthony took his rod and began searching for this saintly ascetic. He walked for an entire day, then fell on his knees to pray. He remained praying throughout the night, and in the morning he got up and continued his journey.

As the sun was setting, he noticed a cave nearby. When he approached it, he found the door closed, so he knelt on the ground and said, "My saintly father, you know who I am and where I am from, and I will not leave this place before seeing you! You who would not refuse the entry of an animal, I ask you, do not refuse me!" Abba Paula then replied from within the cave, "No one asks for charity by scolding, but rather by weeping."

Abba Anthony remained kneeling at the entrance of the cave for a long while, before finally Abba Paula opened the door for him. The two fathers embraced, then prayed together.

As they spoke about the many wonders of God, a raven flew passed and dropped a loaf of bread before them. Abba

Paula held the loaf of bread reverently, and turned to Abba Anthony saying, "Blessed is the Lord my God; for eighty years He has provided for me half a loaf of bread daily, but today because of your presence, He has given us a full loaf! Blessed is the Lord, who satisfies the needs of my body!" Together they once again stood to pray before eating.

They spent the entire night praising God, until the morning sun dawned. Abba Anthony then said to Abba Paula, "Blessed is the hour in which God made me worthy of seeing you my father." Abba Paula replied, "Anthony, return now to your cave and come back to me with the gown Pope Athanasius will give you, for with it you must wrap my body for burial; so go quickly, for the hour of my departure has come!" Abba Paula blessed and prayed for Abba Anthony, and then they embraced each other before departing.

Abba Anthony returned to his monastery after a two day journey through the wilderness. His disciples who were very worried about him being gone so long, rejoiced when they saw him. They ran towards him asking, "Father, where were you?" to which he replied, "I am a sinner and unworthy, for indeed the Lord has revealed to me someone much greater than I."

Taking the gown given to him by Pope Athanasius, Abba Anthony returned to the saintly father's cave. On arrival he saw a host of angels carrying the soul of the blessed saint Abba Paula. Abba Anthony entered his cave and found the saint lying on the ground with his hands outstretched like a cross. He wept bitterly. He then carefully wrapped the pure saint's body within the gown, and prayed over him with heartfelt tears.

As he was wondering how he was going to dig a grave for the saint's blessed body, two lions entered the cave, knelt down beside Abba Paula's body and kissed him. They then turned and began licking the feet of Abba Anthony as if to say, 'where shall we dig?' Abba Anthony drew the sign of the cross on the ground inside the cave, and immediately the lions began digging. After Abba Anthony placed Abba Paula's body within the grave, he took his garment made from weaved palm, and went back to the Patriarch Abba Athanasius and told him all that he had seen and experienced of the life of the great Abba Paula. The Patriarch took Abba Paula's garment as a blessing and only wore it three times a year : on the feast of Epiphany, Easter and the Ascension of our gracious Saviour.

Pope Athanasius had the thought of bringing back from the wilderness the body of Abba Paula so that he may rest beside the body of Pope Ananious. So Abba Anthony, together with some priests went in search for Abba Paula's cave. After two days of wandering through the wilderness, they became disoriented and were unable to find the saint's cave. Abba Paula then appeared to Abba Athanasius in a vision saying, "Send word for the fathers to return from their search, because it is God's will that no one find my body." Immediately the Patriarch sent forth Abba Olgious that he might convey Abba Paula's message to the fathers, so that they may return from the wilderness.

Pope Athanasius wrote the life story of Abba Paula and placed it in the church of Alexandria, so that it may be a blessing and inspiration to all those seeking monasticism.

There was once a boy called Aladnos from Alexandria who fell terribly sick and died. Pope Athanasius said, "I took the garment which Abba Paula used to wear and placed it over the boy's body; immediately he arose, and I personally witnessed this."

Abba Paula lived to be over one hundred and ten years old, during which time he spent more than eighty years as an ascetic dwelling in the Eastern Wilderness.

The Hermit Fathers

The monastery of Abba Paula in the Eastern Wilderness was built in the 4th century, and to this day is the home for a community of monks. It is situated to the south east of the monastery of Abba Anthony. Both these monasteries are located in the centre of Boash, which is a town proceeding the province of Bani-Suweif.

Abba Anthony and Abba Paula are inseparable friends. They are found standing together in icons, mentioned together in Doxologies, and in the Liturgy's commemoration : "...our righteous father Abba Anthony the great, the upright Abba Paula..."

The church celebrates the feast of Abba Paula each year on the 2nd day of the blessed Coptic month Amsheer.

"Hail to our father Anthony the light of monasticism, hail to our father Pavli beloved of Christ..."

(From the Verse of the Cymbals)

20. ABBA NOUFER THE HERMIT

Abba Bebnoda once said: I wanted to venture into the inner wilderness for the sake of receiving the blessings of the hermit fathers. I took some bread and water and walked for four days.

My bread and water had finished, but I continued walking for a further four days until I was fraught with fear and the thought that I was going to die. With the little strength that was left in me, I stood to pray. With the Lord's encouragement, I continued walking for a few more days until I became extremely hungry and thirsty, and in exhaustion I fell to the ground. I opened my eyes and found a person standing before me. He touched my lips with his fingertips and immediately my strength was renewed.

After walking continuously for another four days, I once again felt drained of any energy, so I lifted up my hands and prayed to the Lord. Before me approached the person I had seen before. Once more he touched my lips and my body and again my strength returned.

After God granted me this wonderful miracle, I journeyed for a further seventeen days within the wilderness. In the distance I noticed a very strange looking man who wore no clothes, but the hair on his body covered him like a cloak. As he approached me, I became very frightened and so I ran to the top of the mountain; I thought that perhaps he may be a mountain lion. He remained at the foot of the mountain, but lifted his face towards me and said, "Come down my brother Bebnoda and do not be afraid, for I am a man like you and I have dwelt in this wilderness for many years because of my love for Christ." I was astonished he knew my name, but felt that indeed he was filled with the Holy Spirit, so at once I descended and knelt before him.

As we sat together, I asked him to tell me about his life. He humbly responded, "My name is Noufer, and I have dwelt in this wilderness for the past sixty years, living in the fear of God. The beasts are my friends and with them I share my cave. I feed upon wild grass and these fruit-bearing trees and you are the first person I have seen in sixty years." After a brief pause, he continued: "I began my spiritual life as a monk in the Barida Monastery where one hundred and forty monks lived together in love and harmony. Daily we ate together and praised together, and the peace of our Lord filled our hearts. At that time, I was still in my youth and diligently I learnt and observed the virtues and wisdom of my saintly fathers, for they resembled the angels of God.

One day I heard my fathers speaking about the desert fathers who dwell within the wilderness. They said that these fathers speak to God as if face to face, just like Elijah and John the Baptist, so curiously I asked, "How could these desert fathers be of higher spirituality than yourselves?" They answered, "My son, they are the ones who are found just and righteous in the sight of God; we are nothing in comparison for we live a communal life - eat and drink when we feel the need, are served when we feel weak and we console one another in times of depression. But as for the desert dwellers, they have none of this. From the start of their ascetic life, they roam the wilderness in the intense heat of the day and the bitter coldness of the night. They suffer from the severity of hunger, thirst and exhaustion, and face relentless spiritual struggles and Satanic wars. But all this they endure patiently and willingly because of their great love for our Lord Jesus Christ and in expectation of their heavenly reward. Because of their perseverance and their strong faith, the Lord sends His angels to administer and serve them, just as it is written in the book of Isaiah the prophet, "Those who wait on the Lord shall renew their strength; they shall mount up with wings like eagles, they shall run and not be weary, they shall walk and not faint...when [they] seek water and there is none...I the Lord will hear them; I the God of

Israel will not forsake them. I will open rivers in desolate heights and fountains in the midst of valleys; I will make the wilderness a pool of water and the dry land springs of water..." (Isaiah 40:31, 41:17-18), and also in the Psalms of King David we are told "The righteous cry, and the Lord hears them and delivers them out of all their troubles" (Ps 34:17).

Abba Noufer then said to me, "Abba Bebnoda, as I heard these words, my heart was enlightened, and so that night I packed enough bread to last me three days and went forth from the monastery in the hope that the Lord will lead me to the place He has chosen for me. As I left the monastery gate by night, I found standing before me a person full of light. I was very frightened and wanted to quickly return to my cell within the monastery. The lighted person approached me saying, "Do not be afraid for I am the angel of the Lord; I have been with you from your childhood, and I will accompany you always." Together we walked side by side for about seven miles through the wilderness.

I then continued journeying alone until I reached a small cave, so I knocked on the door and said, "Bless me my father!" A saintly father with the face of an angel emerged from within the cave with a warm smile. I knelt at his feet, but he raised me up saying, "May the Lord bless you my dear friend Noufer, please come in." I remained with him for a few days in order to learn and benefit from his spirituality and wisdom. He taught me how I should spend my time each day and he strengthened and forewarned me of the Satanic wars which I shall face. Finally he said to me, "My son, you too must face spiritual struggles, so arise and venture deep within the inner wilderness, and there spend your time in prayer and praise, for the Lord has called you to live an ascetic life."

The saintly father accompanied me for four days until we found a deserted fortress and beside it was a fruit bearing palm tree. He turned to me and said, "Noufer, this is the place which

God has chosen for you to serve Him in." The hermit father remained with me for a month, during which time he instructed me in the ways of virtues and godly deeds which I was to apply in my life of ascetism.

We continued meeting one another once a year, until he passed away to the Heavenly Kingdom. I buried him with great respect and reverence in the place where he spent his life worshipping God.

I Bebnoda then asked Abba Noufer, "Did you face any trials or hardships when you began your life of hermitage in the wilderness?" to which he replied, "Believe me my beloved brother, I have faced death many times; from hunger, thirst, extremes in temperature to the extent that my body withered, but I was patient and endured all things. Many times the devil would appear and torment me, but my Lord Jesus Christ, blessed be His name, would comfort me and save me from the traps of the enemy. This palm tree produces twelve baskets of dates a year, and each basket feeds me for a month. I also eat wild grass and because of God's great love, He makes the grass taste as sweet as honey in my mouth. Now my brother Bebnoda, let us go to the place where I live."

We walked for about three miles through the wilderness until we reached his fortress, and its nearby palm tree. After we stood to pray, we sat together and spoke about the many wonders of God. As the sun began to set, I saw before the entrance of the fortress a loaf of bread and a jug of water. Abba Noufer said to me, "Get up my brother and eat this bread and drink this water, for you have suffered greatly along the way to find me." We shared the meal and even though we ate until we were satisfied, there was plenty left over. We then stood to pray and remained praying throughout the night.

The following day I looked at Abba Noufer's face and found it had become like fire. I was very frightened, but he turned to me and said, "Do not be afraid brother Bebnoda, for our beloved Lord Jesus Christ has sent you to me so that you may take care of and bury my body, for the hour of my deliverance quickly approaches." I Bebnoda then asked him, "Father, do you think that the Lord will make me worthy enough to live within your dwelling place after your blessed departure?" But he replied, "My dear son, the only reason the Lord had in leading you here is to bury my body, and then return to your monastery to tell your fellow brothers the monks all the wonders you have seen, for in so doing they may praise and glorify our Father in heaven." I knelt before him and said, "Bless me my saintly father; may God be merciful to me and make me worthy of seeing you once again in His Heavenly Kingdom."

Abba Noufer remained praying on me for a long while, then he turned to pray for himself with many tears before lying on the ground with his hands outstretched, and quietly he released his spirit. It was the 16th day of the blessed month of Baouna, and I Bebnoda saw before me a whole host of angels praising and singing as they carried the soul of the pure saint Abba Noufer saying, "Pure is your soul Noufer, for it is without blemish; so let us present it as a beautiful 'korban' to Christ our Lord, the King of Glory!" Immediately I took the tunic I was wearing and tore it in two. I wrapped the body of the blessed father Abba Noufer with one piece, and covered myself with the other. I placed his body in a small stone cave, and prayed on him before sealing the cave's entrance.

The same hour Abba Noufer departed, the palm tree withered and fell, and the fortress which was his home crumbled to the ground. It was then that I realised the strength of Abba Noufer's words when he told me that it was not God's will that I remain in his place.

I ate the bread which was left over from the meal we shared together and drank the rest of the water. I then stood to pray before returning to the monastery. Suddenly, the person who had come to me at the beginning of my journey and touched my lips, again returned to me. He strengthened and encouraged me and so I left Abba Noufer's blessed place glorifying the Lord through His beloved saint Abba Noufer the hermit.

May his blessings be with us all, amen.

21. ABBA GHALEON THE HERMIT

Abba Issac, the abbot of El Kalamon Monastery once said:
There was a saint called Ghaleon who used to reside in
this monastery. He was brought up in one of the villages in
Upper Egypt, and God granted him the gift of performing
miracles and healing the sick. He prayed and fasted diligently;
only eating once a week. He was chosen to be the reader in
the monastery, because he had a clear, strong voice. He
read many church books and so became spiritually
knowledgeable and wise. He also possessed many virtues.

He was consecrated as a monk while he was still in his youth,
but took his spiritual life very seriously. He lived an ascetic life
within his own cell, and only came out during prayer times.
Daily the young saint increased in the love and fear of
God, until the devil could no longer tolerate his
spirituality and virtues. He therefore appeared to him as he
was on his way to midnight prayers, disguised as a hermit
saying, "Brother Ghaleon, I am one of twelve desert
fathers who dwell in the wilderness. Today, however, one of
my fellow desert dwellers passed away. Of course you realise
that once one of the desert fathers die, he must be replaced,
and so we are asking you brother Ghaleon, because of your
love for solitude, to leave this monastery and come dwell with
us in the wilderness." Having said this, the devil then vanished.

The vision was so convincing that Ghaleon believed the Lord
had sent His angel to deliver this message, and that it must have
been God's will. Ghaleon began praying for this situation,
and after the midnight prayers, he took his rod and quickly
left from the monastery gate. He found before him eleven
monks who approached and greeted him. He then followed
closely behind them as they walked through the wilderness
amidst the darkness of the night. They continued walking
until midday when they reached a very high mountain, where
no person, no food and no water was in sight. Suddenly the

eleven monks began laughing wickedly saying, "We have hunted well tonight!" Then Ghaleon thought to himself, "These men could not be saints, but seem to be devils!" He quickly crossed himself and immediately the devils vanished from his sight.

Ghaleon remained on the mountain feeling frightened and lost, and so began praying the Psalms of David: "I will love You O Lord my strength. The Lord is my rock and my fortress" (Ps18). After praying this psalm three times, his fears were calmed and his heart was comforted. He looked around him and when he found no one, he began praying Psalm 6: "O Lord, do not rebuke me in Your anger...have mercy on me O Lord, heal me for my bones are troubled, and my soul is greatly troubled..!" He then lifted his hands towards heaven and prayed, "Make haste O God to deliver me, make haste to help me O Lord..!" (Ps70), then, "May the Lord answer you in the day of trouble. May the name of the God of Jacob defend you. May He send you help from His sanctuary..." (Ps20). Still being filled with despair he continued, "I will lift up my eyes to the hills, from whence comes my help? My help comes from the Lord who made heaven and earth..." (Ps121). Suddenly as he finished praying this psalm, he heard angelic voices in the distance. Quickly he turned and saw three monks clothed in white garments approaching him while praising Psalm 97: "O sing to the Lord a new song for He has done marvellous things..!" Their voices resembled the voices of angels, and Ghaleon recognising the tune joined in their praising.

Because of his last experience, he had some doubt as to whether these monks were from God or not, but realising that demons could never utter the beautiful Psalms of David, his fears were put to rest. The four of them stood praying and praising from the psalms throughout the entire night, and when morning had dawned, they sat together and Ghaleon asked them where they were from : "We are monks from the monastery of Abba Shenouda the Archimandrite, but we are desert wanderers. It is not necessary for you to tell us your story, for it has been revealed to us by the Spirit that you have fallen victim to Satan's trap. So let us give thanks to our beloved Lord for His mercy and care."

At the foot of the mountain, they found a spring of fresh water which had been extracted from rocks, and within this spring the Lord supplied them with fish. They took a fish and left it in the sun for a few days to cook before eating it.

Abba Ghaleon remained with these saintly fathers at the foot of the mountain for a year, then one night one of the three monks said, "Ghaleon, your spiritual father Abba Issac is praying to God that he may see you before your death, so arise quickly and return to him." Ghaleon replied, "But father, I do not know the way!" Immediately, the desert father took Ghaleon by the hand and said, "Follow us." He followed them closely and before dawn he found himself standing at the door of the monastery. The three monks farewelled him before returning to their monastery of Abba Shenouda the Archimandrite.

"When Ghaleon entered the monastery, my heart rejoiced exceedingly and so I Issac embraced him saying, 'My dear son Ghaleon, where have you been?' So he began to tell me his story..."

After he had finished speaking, I Issac said to him, "Let me tell you what the Lord has revealed to me regarding you: when you were away in the wilderness, I prayed that God would tell me of your whereabouts, for I was worried about you. Then in my dream I saw someone saying to me, "Do not be concerned, for today you shall see Ghaleon in the flesh, and seven days later he will leave this world to enjoy eternal life with Jesus Christ, so take care not to forget this day!" Since you left this monastery my son Ghaleon, there has been no other like you; no one who reads like you or memorises the church songs and psalms like you. For this reason, I cried bitterly when I could not find you." There was a bright young boy called Moses whose love for God was great. He became the monastery's reader after Abba Ghaleon, so I presented him to Ghaleon and said, "Teach him the rites of the church and all the hymns", so he took the boy Moses and embraced him closely saying, "My son Moses, accept the Spirit who dwells in me, for on the seventh day I will pass away." And having said this, he breathed on him.

Moses eagerly learnt from Abba Ghaleon and increased in the knowledge of church hymns and spiritual readings.

On the seventh day the blessed saint Abba Ghaleon delivered his pure soul to the Heavenly King. All the monastery fathers gathered together to pray on him and prepare his body for burial with all due reverence and honour.

To our Lord be all glory forever and ever, amen.

22. ABBA KARAS THE HERMIT

Abba Karas lived at the turn of the 6th century and was the brother of the great King Theodosious. Abba Karas' life story was written by Abba Bemwa; the one who buried the body of St. Elaria, the daughter of King Zenon. (He is not to be confused, however, with Abba Bemwa, the teacher of the two saintly fathers Abba Bishoy and Abba John the Short).

This is Abba Karas' story, as was recorded by Abba Bemwa: One day I heard a voice saying to me, "Go quickly into the inner wilderness, for there you will meet Abba Karas who is greatly honoured by our Lord Jesus Christ because of the many hardships he has endured for the sake of His Holy Name." Immediately I got up and ventured into the wilderness, in search of the saintly father. I continued walking for many days without seeing anyone, and finally I noticed a nearby cave. I approached and knocked its door saying, "Bless me my father the saint!" I then heard the reply, "Blessed is your coming to me today Abba Bemwa, the priest of Sheheet, and the one whom God made worthy of burying the body of the pure saint Elaria, daughter of King Zenon!" I was greatly surprised at his response and his knowledge of my name, and when he opened his door, I quietly entered.

He greeted me warmly, then we sat down together and spoke about the many wonders and glories of God. I marvelled at the strictness of his ascetism, and so I said to him, "Father, are there any other hermit fathers who dwell in this wilderness?" He sighed deeply and said, "There is one who dwells among us, whose footsteps the world is not worthy of, and his name is Abba Karas." I asked this blessed father sitting before me, "What is your name and what is your story?" to which he replied, "My name is Simon, and you are the first human I have seen in sixty years...I eat every Saturday, when God in His infinite love, provides me with a loaf of bread delivered on the doorstep to my cave..." After receiving Abba Simon's many blessings, I asked him to pray for me, before continuing my journey.

I walked for three days before seeing another cave, and when I approached and knocked I heard a voice from within saying, "Blessed is your coming to me today Abba Bemwa!" and again I was greatly surprised. I asked him the same question I had previously asked Abba Simon, and he replied, "There lives one in the wilderness, whom the whole world is not worthy of. He speaks with God and God listens." I asked him, "Father, are you the blessed Abba Karas?" Humbly he answered, "Who am I to hear such words? I am but very poor and in no way comparable to Abba Karas, the friend of angels!...I am Bamon and I have dwelt in this wilderness for twenty nine years, feeding on the fruits of this palm tree..." Once again, I asked this saintly father for his blessings before continuing with my search.

As I journeyed within the inner wilderness, I heard a great voice which frightened me, and then all of a sudden I found myself standing at the entrance of a cave. I knocked its door and once more I heard the response, "Blessed is your coming to me today Abba Bemwa!" I entered and found before me a man who had the face of an angel. He had a long white beard and from him shone rays as bright as the sun. He looked very fragile and spoke in a soft voice. I knelt before him and said, "Hail to you my father the saint." He looked at me with gentle eyes and said, "My beloved brother, I have been waiting for you a long time, for with your coming today the Lord has permitted my departure." We sat together and I asked him to tell me about his life...

"My name is Karas, and I have dwelt in this wilderness for fifty seven years, during which time I have not seen a fellow human..."

As the sun began to set my blessed father Karas was suddenly struck by a severe fever, and in pain he kept sighing, "How can I escape Your judgement O Lord, and from Your Spirit where can I hide? O my Lord, how I fear the hour! Be merciful to me O Lord, because of my many sins!" I Bemwa marvelled at his words, for he was a great and saintly hermit father!

On the 7th of Abib I found my father Abba Karas still feverish, but amidst his pain, his eyes were uplifted towards heaven, calmly, for a long time. He then said to me, "My beloved brother, one of our greatest pillars has passed away today in Upper Egypt. Indeed the world has lost a great saint, whom no one was worthy of his footstep, and he is Abba Shenouda the Archimandrite. But now he is resting in peace with our Lord."

His illness was becoming progressively more severe, and on the 8th day of the blessed month of Abib, Abba Karas' angelic face shone brightly, and at midday an unbearably strong, bright light illuminated the cave, and there standing before us was our Lord God and Saviour Jesus Christ, glory be to Him, together with the Archangels Michael and Gabriel and a host of angels praising and singing. As the Lord of glory approached the pure saint, Abba Karas said to Him, "My Lord and God, I ask You, for my sake to please bless Your servant Bemwa who has come to me from afar." So the Lord, glory be to Him, turned to me and said, "My peace be with you Bemwa, and My blessing come upon you." He then turned to Abba Karas and said, "Do not be sad My beloved one; death for you is not death but eternal life and transformation from this passing world to the place of eternal joy and perfection." Our blessed Saviour then took unto Him the soul of the pure saint Abba Karas.

I wrapped the body of the saint in cloth, and then left his cave. At the entrance, the Lord of glory, placed His hand on the cave to bless it, and suddenly it was as if the cave had no door. He bestowed upon me His peace, before ascending in great glory. On my return to the monastery, I passed by the caves of Abba Bamon and Abba Simon, and eventually I reached Sheheet. I told all the fathers about Abba Karas, whose life story is as sweet smelling incense to all those who hear it; for the Lord is glorified through His saints.

Our church celebrates the feast of Abba Karas on the 8th of Abib each year. He is also mentioned in the church 'Tasbeha' and the Liturgy's Commemoration.

May his blessings be with us all, amen.

23. ABBA MISAEL THE HERMIT

Abba Issac, the abbot of El Kalamon monastery tells us this story:

One Sunday morning, I was present in the monastery church when behind me I heard a young voice saying, "Father Issac, please accept me as one of your sons, and clothe me in the 'eskeem' of monasticism; for I know you have the authority to do this, because I have seen how obedient the monks are to you." Before me stood a boy of about twelve years old, but I felt he possessed many spiritual fruits, and that he came seeking the life of worship with all his heart. I said to him, "My son, go and remain within one of the monastery cells for a while, and if you are patient and strong enough to overcome trials and temptations through constant praying and living in solitude, then you can be a monk." I also advised him to study spiritual books and church history books, as well as memorise all the psalms. I asked one of the monastery fathers to stay close by him and teach him the rites of monasticism.

Curious about this young boy, I asked him, "My son, you are still very young; perhaps you have disobeyed your parents and so escaped from them to come here. Please tell me about yourself."

"My parents were very evil; they never prayed and never had compassion for others. They were becoming advanced in years and because they could not bear any children, they were deeply distressed. Eventually they spoke to a monk priest about their situation, and he answered them saying, "Firstly, you must go and repent, and then God will give you a son." That same moment, they repented, prayed diligently and comforted the poor. They asked their village priest to teach them how to pray, and he asked them to memorise Psalm 50: "Have mercy upon me O Lord according to your loving kindness..." Finally God granted them a child. They brought me up in love and in the fear of God. They had in their possessions many things - cows, goats, furniture, and all this they gave away to the poor.

When I was five years old, my father died, and one year later my mother followed, and so I was left alone. One day I thought to myself, "Where is my father now and where is my mother? And where are all those people who died before them?" I realised that this world on earth will not last forever, and so I decided to escape into the wilderness..."

Abba Issac then continued: "Before a year had passed, the boy had learnt all the church doctrines, memorised all the spiritual books, and he fasted and prayed diligently. His guardian father came to me one day and said, "Indeed father, this boy is filled with the grace of the Holy Spirit."

When I felt that he had endured all trials patiently, and when I saw the fervencies of his prayers, I clothed him with the 'eskeem' of monasticism, and named him Misael, and at that very moment, his face shone brightly with the light and grace of the Holy Spirit. He lived an ascetic life in his cell, to the extent that no one realised his existence. Then one night, one of the monks came to me saying, "Father I have heard the voice of a man blaming himself saying, 'O my soul, realise now that the human body always desires the lusts of the world, and this is the result of sin, therefore, if you seek salvation, escape from sin.'" I the weak Issac realised that the devil was enticing our young monk with worldly cares...

So I then went to see Abba Misael. When I approached his cell, I found that he had not yet finished his midnight prayers, so I remained outside his door until he finished. He then welcomed me into his cell and I asked, "My dear son, has anything happened to you tonight? Has the enemy disturbed you?" Kneeling before me he said, "Father, the devil knows my whereabouts, but he cannot tolerate hearing my prayers." I noticed that he was reading from the book of Solomon, and I was assured that Misael was too one of great wisdom.

One day I went to visit him in his cell, and when I stood at his door, I found him praying, "Do not leave me, nor forsake me O God of my salvation. When my father and mother forsake me, then the Lord will take care of me" (Ps27). I knocked his door, and he warmly welcomed me. I found his body had become like dry wood, unlike when he first entered the monastery. His hands and feet had become slender like the stem of a palm, and nothing of his body seemed to be left except for his bright eyes with which he kindly stared at me. He said to me, "Father Issac, you must rejoice!" So I replied crying, "How can I do such a thing! When you entered the monastery you were a beautiful healthy boy, but now look, you have become like the dead!" Misael answered me lovingly, "During these years, God never dimmed my eyes, but strengthened me so that I may stand to pray. This body seeks the world and its desires, but I have prevented and restricted it from such things and for this reason, my body has become as you see it." I realised the greatness of this blessed saint standing before me and the heights of his spirituality, and therefore I asked him to pray for me...

Having done this, he looked at me with gentle eyes and said, "Father, shall I tell you what I saw in my sleep? After three days men from the Port of Alexandria will come to this monastery, demanding one of your monks. Do not forbid them, lest they bring sorrow to the monastery and kill the monks, for they are powerful men and are sent by the king." Misael then began to cry, "Father, I am the monk they must take away, but please do not be sad for God is with me; He is my protector, but be sure that I will return to you. The following year there will be a disaster on earth, but do not be afraid; I will come to you, and you shall see the will of God revealed." I was greatly perplexed at what he was saying, so I shared his dream with my fellow brethren, and they too were surprised.

A few days later, a group of men from the Port of Alexandria came to the monastery with a letter, and imprinted in the letter was the name of the blessed saint Misael. They said aggressively, "Bring this man to us for we will not permit him to remain in this place another day!" I was greatly distressed and so replied "I do not know this monk; he is not here." Immediately they bound me with a metal chain and tied me to a marble pillar. They drove all the monks out of the monastery and wanted to take me back to Alexandria, when suddenly Abba Misael stood before them asking, "Whom do you seek?" They replied, "The young monk Misael, for the king has need of him!" He then said, "Leave this old man, and I shall lead you to him." They untied me the weak Jacob and left me behind, and took the blessed saint Abba Misael. They left the monastery and I never saw him again. The brethren and I cried bitterly for days...

A year later, there was a great famine and many people died because of lack of food, but because the saintly father had forewarned me, I gathered large amounts of wheat, maize, oats and beans and stored them in the monastery. This kept us safe throughout the days of the great famine.

When the governor heard we had food stored in the monastery, he came begging for food. Eventually, demand increased and so in fear I cried remembering the saint's words, "I will come to you during the famine."

The governor and all his people began consuming our food in great amounts. Suddenly a group of men came to the monastery and said to the governor, "What are you doing here in this wilderness?" to which he replied, "Food! they have food here that is nowhere else to be found in all the earth!" Immediately they said, "Leave this monastery at once and do not return, lest you die by the sword!" Quickly, the governor and all his men got up and left, and no harm came to the monastery.

I Issac was eager to know who these men were, and when I offered them food to eat they said, "No, you are the one in need of food." I approached the elder of the group and said, "Brother please tell me, where are you from?" One of the fathers answered, "The king has given us the responsibility to take care of this wilderness and to make sure that no harm comes to its dwellers." I fell to the ground before them and begged them to tell me who they are, but as I looked up, I found they had departed into the wilderness, so I pondered over what I had seen and heard...

A younger looking man remained behind. He came towards me, took my hand and sat in front of me saying, "My dear Father Issac, truly God has been most merciful to me; for I am your son Misael whom you clothed with the 'eskeem' of monasticism. The men who were just with me are the same men who took me away from you and none of my monastery brothers have seen me since; just as I had told you beforehand. The men whom you have recently seen are heavenly members, and the city which they claimed to be from - Alexandria, is actually Jerusalem. Together with them I ventured through the wilderness and other places where there are those who live in obedience and in the fear of God." I Issac then asked, "Dear brother, can I join you so that I may rest from my pastoral responsibilities in the monastery, for there are many other shepherds." But Abba Misael replied, "Father this cannot be so, for you have been given authority from heaven to care for the monastery brothers and to lead them spiritually, so do not be afraid Father Issac." He comforted me with his many beautiful words of spiritual benefit, and then he asked me about his fellow monastery brothers. He asked me to send each one of them his greetings and then said, "Go to

Abba Athanasius, the bishop of my hometown and take from him the remainder of the money which my parents left for me, for it has been kept in his care, and build a church within this monastery which will bear my name." Having said this, he left me and caught up with his friends...

After this incident, I went straight to my father the bishop, just as Abba Misael had requested of me. The Bishop Athanasius gave me two times 900 pounds of gold, 400 pieces of woollen cloth, 100 layers of sheepskin and 500 horses. I was astonished by all these possessions.

I returned to the monastery and converted his cell into a beautiful church. The day arrived in which his church was to be consecrated. Great crowds gathered from the monasteries and towns in Upper Egypt; the Bishop of Fao was present, along with many other bishops, monks and priests. When the prayers for consecration had begun, I saw before me the same group of fathers I had seen previously. They entered the church with rods in their hands and from their rods came beams of light in the shape of crosses. Although I could see them standing before me, no one else did. I approached them, knelt before them and asked that they pray for me. I then went to my beloved son Misael and greeted him.

They remained in the church until the ceremony had finished and all the people had left. The groups of fathers then followed, but Abba Misael remained behind. He came towards me and said, "Father Issac, prepare for yourself a tomb in this church, for on this day next year you shall go to God's holy place which the Lord has prepared for you."

Abba Misael then departed from me and I never saw him again. I arranged for my tomb to be built at the north side of this church.

I Issac saw and knew Abba Misael from his childhood. He lived in obedience to God's commandments and complete self-denial of all worldly and bodily desires and pleasures. He was like an angel; praising and praying unceasingly.

The church of Abba Misael the hermit is still present in Abba Samuel's Monastery in El Kalamon, and was consecrated on the 10th day of the Coptic month Bashans, in the year 396 A.D., during the reign of Diocletian.

Our church celebrates his feast each year on the 13th day of the blessed Coptic month of Kiakh. May his blessings be with us all.

Glory be to our Holy Trinity, now and forever, amen.

24. ST MARY THE HERMIT

In the 4th century lived an ascetic monk priest by the name of Father Zocima who was from a monastery in Palestine. The monastery's location was not far from the wilderness where our Lord Jesus Christ fasted for forty days and nights. It is a monastic custom that each year the monks would spend the spiritual days of Lent in solitude outside of the monastery.

It was the first Sunday of the Great Lent, when Abba Zocima ventured into the wilderness to spend the forty days in spiritual retreat. After these holy days were over, Abba Zocima was walking back to the monastery when he noticed a human form quickly pass him by. He made the sign of the cross and carefully approached the figure...he then heard a voice saying, "Give me your cape so that I may cover my nakedness, for I am a woman." She knelt before Abba Zocima and said, "Bless me Abba Zocima, for you are a priest of God." After he prayed for her, he asked that she reveal her story...

"I was born in Egypt in the year 344. When I was twelve years old, I disobeyed my father's wish and travelled to Alexandria; I am ashamed to think how I first lost my virginity there, and how I was set on fire with the endless desire for pleasure. I was exposed to many harmful things, that at such an early age, destroyed the purity of my mind. I then became curious to experience many things, and so I willingly surrendered myself to lusts and bodily desires. As a result, I lost my virginity at the age of seventeen.

While I was living in this way, one summer I saw a great crowd of men going down toward the sea. I stopped one of them and asked him where they were going, and he said, "We are all going to Jerusalem to celebrate the feast of the Holy Cross." Drawn by curiosity, I joined the pilgrims going by ship to Jerusalem. On the way I seduced many of my companions, and I continued to live in this way in Jerusalem.

As the feast day of the Holy Cross approached, I wanted to enter the church like everyone else, but this mysterious force prevented me. The more I persisted in trying to enter, the more it would throw me back. Giving up, I sat in a lonely place not far from the church and wondered about this strange experience. I then thought to myself, 'it must be because I am a sinner and unworthy of entering such a place, for what relation is there between an evil one such as myself, and the cross of the Lord Jesus?' Suddenly guilt filled my heart and I began to cry bitterly while beating on my chest. I then carefully approached the icon of St. Mary and said, "Was not your Son incarnated for the salvation of sinners? If this is so, please help me! O faithful pleader, ask your Son to make me worthy of entering His church so that I may throw myself before His Holy Cross. Save me from this power that resists my entry, and I promise never to return to my worldly and sinful life, with all its desires and pleasures, and I shall go wherever the Lord leads me!"

After finishing my prayers of repentance, the Lord permitted that I enter into His holy church. I felt so shameful and unworthy before His greatness and majesty, that slowly I approached His Holy Cross and fell to the ground before it weeping bitterly.

I lost track of time during my prayers, and when I lifted my head, I found it was midday. I left the church glorifying the Lord saying, "Glory be to you my Lord, God and Saviour, who accepted the pleadings of Your mother on my behalf, for You have accepted me, just as You accept all sinners who return to You. I cannot comprehend the compassion and unlimited love and the new life You grant to those who repent! And as for you blessed Virgin Mother, pray to your Son for me, that He may lead me along the paths of righteousness, and now my Master and Lord, into Your hands do I surrender my life." I then heard a voice saying, "Cross the River Jordan and there you will find the place of your salvation." On the way a man gave me three pieces of silver with which to buy bread. I bought three loaves and took them with me on my journey. I was then twenty nine years old, and now it has been forty five years since I left the holy city Jerusalem.

I reached the church of St. John the Baptist which is located near the Jordan. The memory of my many sins still haunted me, so I washed my face in the river before entering the holy place and confessing my sins to the priest. When the father absolved me, I felt an incredible relief; it was as though a burden had been lifted! I then completed my joy by receiving the Holy Sacraments.

I left the church and fed on a little of the bread I had with me. I continued walking for two days without eating. I then stopped a while to rest before sailing by boat to the other side of the Jordan River...

The trials and satanic wars I faced were severe, and to this day I remember them and tremble. For seventeen years the devil stirred within me disturbing and lustful desires. Many times I hungered and thirsted, which brought about memories of my past, and I craved to taste the sweet liquors I was once so accustomed to drinking...Many secular songs filled my mind, and then I would beat on my chest remembering the day of my repentance, and once again surrender myself with tears of repentance before the Lord, asking for the pleadings of His Virgin Mother St. May.

After relentless spiritual struggles and many tears, a bright light would surround me and immediately the devil would flee. I would then live in the comfort and security of God's glory...

When I had eaten the three loaves of bread I had with me, I began eating from the grass of the wilderness...my clothes wore out and my body was burnt many times from the extreme heat of the sun, and trembled greatly from the cold desert nights, but God in His infinite love preserved me so that my heart rejoiced exceedingly. Father, you are the first person I have seen since crossing the Jordan River many years ago, so I ask you to pray for me." She knelt before Abba Zocima to take his blessings, and he lifted up his hands towards heaven saying, "Blessed are You O God in the highest, who is the performer of great miracles. Blessed is Your holy name, for You have revealed to me the many treasures of Your grace."

St. Mary said to him, "Father, please do not tell anyone about me before my death. Now, you must return to your monastery in peace. The following year you will not be able to come to me during the days of Lent, for this is God's will, but come and meet me on the shores of the Jordan on Holy Thursday, and bring for me the Holy Body and Blood of my Lord Jesus Christ. Abba Zocima, I ask you to tell Abba John the abbot of your monastery to keep close watch over his flock, for they are in need of care and discipline. And finally, do not forget to pray for me."

Abba Zocima returned to his monastery on Palm Sunday, and kept in his heart all that he had seen and heard, just as St. Mary requested of him. The following year, he was unable to leave the monastery during Lent because he was struck by a severe fever. He then remembered St. Mary's words, and realised that his illness was the will of God.

After the Holy Mass on Holy Thursday, Abba Zocima carefully carried the Holy Sacraments, and took with him some vegetables and went out seeking the blessed saint Mary. When he reached the shores of the Jordan River, he saw the saint in the distance making the sign of the cross on the water, then walked upon it until she stood before him. She knelt before the Holy Body and Blood of Christ in complete reverence and prayed the Orthodox Creed and the Lord's Prayer before receiving the Holy Sacraments.

She then said to Abba Zocima, "By the will of God, come to me next year, and meet me at the cave where you first saw me." He prayed for her before she once again made the sign of the cross on the water and crossed over, returning to her cave.

The following year, the saintly father Zocima went to the cave of St. Mary and found her kneeling towards the east; she had already passed away. Abba Zocima fell to the ground crying, then as he got up to pray, he noticed a message engraved beside her: "Abba Zocima, bury the body of Mary the Repentant in this place and leave this body of sin for the dust." Abba Zocima was comforted by this message and marvelled when he saw a lion sitting by guarding her body. When he became worried as to how to dig a grave for her, the lion which sat guarding the body began digging. Abba Zocima then prayed over the body of St. Mary the hermit, before burying her and placing the sign of the cross on her cave.

Abba Zocima returned to his monastery praising and glorifying God's holy name. He gathered together all the monks of the monastery and told them the beautiful story of the repentance of the pure saint Mary the hermit. Her aromatic story is a comforting and encouraging meditation on God's mercies for all those who struggle in the life of purity and virtues. Abba Zocima kept returning to her cave each year during the days of Holy Lent, until he rested in peace at the age of one hundred. As for St. Mary the hermit, her pure body was discovered during the leadership of Pope John, Patriarch of Jerusalem. Through her, many miracles have occurred. She died in the year 421AD at the age of seventy six. Our church celebrates her feast each year on the 6th day of the blessed Coptic month Baramudah.

May her blessings be with us all, and glory be to God forever, amen.

25. ABBA YOUSAB THE HERMIT

The saintly father Abba Yousab lived in the wilderness of Sheheet. He was well advanced in age, and his body had become weak from his constant spiritual struggles, devotion and strict ascetism. He prayed unceasingly and kept watch throughout the night. He was a blessed man of patience and tolerance, and humbly clothed himself in a tunic of weaved palm. God provided him with food, and upon the soft clouds Abba Yousab would travel from place to place...He possessed many spiritual virtues.

One day he thought curiously to himself, "I wonder if anyone is equal to me in virtues?" and he prayed that the Lord would reveal a sign. Abba Yousab then heard the voice of the Lord's angel saying to him, "He who is the king of Antioch, go to him and see the honour bestowed upon him."

Abba Yousab at once rode upon the clouds, and when he had reached the city of Antioch, he walked with his rod until he arrived at the gate of the city. There he saw the king mounted on his horse, and surrounded by all his soldiers and guards. He was received by all the people with great honour and dignity. The king was clothed in the most exquisite gown, and on his head he wore a crown glittering with diamonds and precious gems. Abba Yousab became very confused at this, and as he wondered how he could compare spiritually with such a magnificent king, the king approached him and said, "Abba Yousab, you bring upon yourself many hardships." He then ordered the soldiers to take the saint to his palace and take care of him there until the king returns.

When the king arrived at the palace, he took hold of the saint's hands and lead him into a lavish hall where a banquet had been prepared. The two of them sat beside each other on the table...Later, the king lead the saint to his private quarters, and there Abba Yousab was introduced to the king's wife. The queen who was arrayed in beautiful jewels and fine apparel, welcomed the saintly father with much joy and warmth. Serving the king and queen were maids who were also very beautifully dressed. Having completed their duties, the queen then dismissed them...

The king and queen then excused themselves and after a short while returned clothed in animal fur. Abba Yousab marvelled at this. They then lead the saint into another room within the palace, and there sitting on the ground, working with his hands was a monk. Immediately the monk came forward to kiss the hermit father, then greeted the king and queen. They then all stood together and prayed the 6th hour prayer, before returning to their craft work. Each one of them worked in silence, then the monk said to the saint, "My saintly father Abba Yousab, it was God's will to reveal to you the life of the king and queen, for it has been a spiritual experience for you." They then spoke about the many wonders of God, His love and His care. After praying the 9th hour prayer, the servant prepared a small table upon which lay bread and a small portion of food. They ate and gave many thanks to God.

The monk then took the saint aside and said, "My dear brother, I hope that you have benefitted from the example of the king and queen, for as you have noticed, their greatness is not in ruling the monarchy, but in spirituality and wisdom. Despite their riches, they live in ascetism and humility. They eat only a little and delight in working with their hands." The king and queen took the saint's blessings before Abba Yousab left, riding upon his cloud back to his cave in El-Eskeet. He glorified God through His chosen people, and lived in joy and continuous prayer and praise until the day he rested in peace.

May all glory be to our God forever, amen.

26. ABBA THOMAS THE HERMIT

Abba Wissa, the disciple of Abba Shenouda the Archimandrite once said :

There lived on the mountain of Shenshif a saintly hermit father called Thomas. He was greatly loved by everyone, and he was a dear friend of my spiritual father. Abba Shenouda used to tell me that there was no other like Abba Thomas in spirituality, and that the Lord Jesus Christ spoke to him, and the angels frequently visited him.

When the hour approached for his departure from this world, he hurried to our wilderness to meet with my father, and together they sat down speaking about the many glories and wonders of God. Abba Thomas said to my father Abba Shenouda: "I shall no longer speak with you in the flesh, for the angel of the Lord has revealed to me this night that my Lord will shortly come to take me with Him. The angel also revealed to me the day of your departure father, so your sons must take note of this day; for it will be on the same day as Alexandria's Archbishop Abba Kyrilos was born, and also the same hour of Abba Boctor's birth, the abbot of Tebansin Monastery. It will be the 7th day of the blessed month of Abib, and many saints will come to you on this day."

My father Abba Shenouda then asked Abba Thomas the hermit, "Father, how will I know the hour of your departure?" to which Abba Thomas replied, "I will give you a sign; the rock on which you sit upon at the entrance of your cave will crack open into two halves, just like an open book. When you see this, then know that my soul has been released from my body. You will see the Archangel Rafael walking before you, together with those whom you choose to accompany you for my burial, and you will reach my dwelling place without any transportation. So I ask you

Abba Shenouda to do this act of love for the sake of God, and bury my body, for I have no one but God alone." My father answered, "let it be according to God's will." They embraced each other for the last time and then the saintly father said to Abba Shenouda, "I will leave you now in the tender care of God, until I meet you again." My father then returned to his cave and daily, he increased in worship and ascetism.

It was three months since my father had spoken with Abba Thomas, and as he stood at the entrance of his cave one morning to pray, he saw the rock before him crack in half; just like an open book. My father sighed deeply and said, "The wilderness of Shenshif had lost its lamp." As he spoke these words, the Archangel Rafael appeared and pointed to Abba Shenouda with his right hand saying, "Hail to you beloved of the Lord, and of all the saints! Come, let us bury the body of the pure saint Thomas, because they are all waiting for you."

My father followed the angel until they arrived at the monastery by nightfall. There Abba Shenouda found a brother praying, "At midnight I will rise to give thanks to You because of Your righteous judgements" (Ps119:62), so my father approached him and said, "Follow me." He then went to Abba Yousab the writer who was praying, "We will rejoice in Your salvation and in the name of our God we will set up our banners" (Ps 20:5), so my father said to him, "Follow me." They approached the strong and courageous Brother Enoch who was praying, "He shall cover you with His feathers, and under His wings you shall take refuge; His truth shall be your shield and buckler" (Ps91:4), and my father said to him, "Follow me." The four of them went into the sanctuary to pray, before leaving the monastery; guided by the Archangel Rafael who walked before them.

Finally they reached the saintly father Abba Thomas' dwelling place, and when they found his body, they fervently prayed on him, wrapped him in cloth and reverently placed him within his cave.

Many miracles were performed through him. The saintly hermit father Abba Thomas rested in peace on the 27th day of the blessed month Bashans, in the year 452AD, and his prophecy about the departure of Abba Shenouda the Archimandrite on the 7th of Abib was fulfilled."

To this day, there is a church which bears the name of the holy saint Abba Thomas the hermit, which is located about five kilometres north of El Sawamaa, north-east of Akhmeem. There is also a monastery in this place which also bears his name.

May his prayers and blessings be with us all, amen.

27. ABBA BEJIMI THE HERMIT

Abba Bejimi was born of poor Christian parents in the town of Fisha, under the bishopric of Masil. When he was twelve years old, he was shepherding his father's flock in the field, when the angel of the Lord appeared to him as a young boy saying, "Would you like to come and be a monk with me, so that we may spend the rest of our lives worshipping God instead of caring for these animals? Three days from now, three monks are coming to take me with them back to their monastery, and if you like you can come too!" The heart of the young boy Bejimi rejoiced exceedingly, for monasticism was his heart's desire, so he said to his new friend, "Yes, please take me with you!"

Three days later, three monks were walking through the field when they sited Bejimi. The angel drew close to them and said, "It is good to take with you this enlightened pillar who will be a shining light in the world, for he is a chosen one of God. He will return to this place in his last days and God will perform many miracles through him, until the day he completes his journey on earth."

Realising that it was the angel of the Lord who was revealing these words to them, the elder of the monks approached the young saint Bejimi and asked, "Would you like to come with us? But I warn you, the journey is long and tiresome." Bejimi answered them, "I shall eagerly follow you." Excitedly, he walked with them until they reached Mount Nitria, and there he rested with them a few days. Then they continued walking within the wilderness of Sheheet for a further seventy miles.

Along the way the monks taught the young Bejimi the rites and traditions of monasticism, and through their example they taught him humility, prayer, fasting, vigils, handiwork and memorising spiritual books. The saint increased daily in spirituality, humility and patience and abiding in the fear of God. The three monastic fathers rejoiced in Bejimi's virtues and good deeds and in his love and dedication in partaking of the holy church sacraments. When he had lived for seven years in obedience and Christian love towards the three monastic fathers, they clothed him in the 'eskeem' of monasticism.

Bejimi was a person who had a beautiful, pleasant appearance, and because of his warm smile and gentleness, they called him the "son of peace." He lived for fifteen years in complete obedience towards the three fathers, until their departure to the Heavenly Kingdom. During the years in which he dwelt with the monastic fathers, they prophesied to him that he would one day become a great spiritual leader. After their departure, Bejimi remained alone in that place for a further two years; thus he dwelt within the wilderness of Sheheet for twenty four years.

His fame spread throughout all the land, and many people and monastic fathers came to see him from all the surrounding regions to receive his blessings. When he found that he was consuming a lot of his time in meeting with people and guiding them spiritually, he became frightened from vain glory and the praise of men, and the evil effect it could have on his heart. So he began meditating on the day of his departure from this world, and the moment of Judgement, and began blaming himself saying, "What can I do if God has need of me this night? How can I stand before God and justify all the deeds I have done in my life?"

He then got up and walked within the wilderness of Sheheet for three days and nights. He took nothing with him except for a palm branch on which he leaned for support. He ate nothing during these three days, and then suddenly devils appeared to him as ferocious beasts, wanting to attack him and eat him, however, they were not able to even approach the saint. So Bejimi said to them, "If my Lord Jesus Christ has given me over to you, then it would not be necessary for all of you to be here, for only one of you would have the strength to kill me, but if the Lord has not given you authority over me, then keep away from me!" and having said this, he made the sign of the cross, and at once they vanished like smoke.

After this incidence, the saint continued walking within the wilderness. He prayed along the way and felt happy that God was beside him and supporting him. After two day of journeying through the wilderness of Sheheet, he came to a small valley filled with beautiful palm trees and a pond of fresh water. He rejoiced when he saw the many animals drinking happily from the pond.

Abba Bejimi then continued walking for a further twenty miles until he found a small cave situated on the side of a high mountain. This was to be his home for the next twenty four years, during which time he lived in strict asceticism, fervent prayer and worship, humility and lowliness of heart; always remembering the Lord's words, "Take My yoke upon you and learn from Me, for I am gentle and lowly in heart, and you will find rest for your souls" (Matthew 11:29).

During the first three years of living in this cave, he ate and drank only once every six days. He ate from the fruits of the palm trees which fell to the ground, and drank fresh spring water. He never stored food or drink in his cave.

Daily he would pray fifty psalms and read from the books of Moses and the prophets. He prostrated four hundred times in the morning, and at night he would kneel and once again pray fifty psalm, together with praising and prayer, reading from many Old Testament books as well as from the Gospels and Epistles.

After three years, his clothes wore out, so he remembered the example of Abba Paula the First Hermit, and weaved for himself a tunic of palms. During these three years, he experienced severe spiritual struggle, so the angel of the Lord appeared to him as a hunter and provided Abba Bejimi with heavenly food; just as the angel had once provided to Elijah the prophet.

Having dwelt in the wilderness for twenty four years, the Lord Jesus Christ, the Archangel Michael and the twelve apostles appeared to Bejimi, and the wilderness was flooded with a brilliant light. The Lord said to the saint, "Peace be with you My chosen one! Because of your love for Me and the sufferings you have endured for Me, a church shall be built in your name..." He then blessed Bejimi and said, "Arise and go to your home town, for there I shall perform many miracles through you, and idol worshippers shall return to the True Faith. There you shall remain for ten years, before completing your life on earth and coming to live with Me in My Heavenly Kingdom forever." Our beloved Lord gave Abba Bejimi His peace and blessing before departing from him. The Archangel Michael then placed the saintly father on a cloud which carried him to a high mountain, three miles from his home town. There Bejimi built a small cave and lived within it in strict ascetism and worship. He was a righteous example to all those who saw him.

A few days later, the angel of the Lord carried him safely to the region of Pharan in Palestine; for it was corrupted by many heresies, but because of the strength of Abba Bejimi's spiritual teachings, and the grace bestowed upon him by the Holy Spirit, he defeated all apostasies. God also granted him the gift of performing miracles, healing the sick and casting out evil spirits.

Abba Bejimi spent five years in the region of Pharan, praying and struggling to bring the lost sheep back into the flock. After the Lord helped him accomplish this, the angel carried him back to the cave near his home town. There he also lived for five years, healing the sick and encouraging many to return to the True Faith. As a result, his fame spread throughout the entire region.

It has been mentioned that Abba Shenouda the Archimandrite saw a vision one night : he lifted up his eyes towards heaven and there he saw a magnificent throne situated upon a pillar of light, and on the throne sat a crown of glittering diamonds. When he asked one of the angels, "Whom does this throne belong to?" the angel replied, "It is for the saintly father Bejimi the hermit, of Fisha in the diocese of Maseal." After this revelation, Abba Shenouda eagerly wanted to see the saint, so he ventured through the wilderness until he found him. The blessed father Abba Bejimi knew by the Spirit who Abba Shenouda was, and so they warmly greeted one another. They spent the entire night praising and praying together, after which they spoke about the many great wonders of God. Abba Shenouda remained with the saint a few days before returning to his monastery.

The Lord revealed to Abba Bejimi the hour of his departure, so he called his disciple to him and gave him a sign by which the hour of his deliverance would be known. It was seven o'clock in the morning on the first day of Kiakh, when the saintly father Abba Bejimi was struck by a severe fever, but in all his pain, he was comforted by a group of saints who came to visit him. On the eleventh day of the blessed month of Kiakh, the holy father Abba Bejimi released his spirit, and a host of angels carried him to the Lord Jesus Christ, who loved him dearly. He was seventy years old when he passed away.

He lived for twelve years in Fisha, seven years in Sheheet with the monastic fathers, seventeen years clothed in the 'eskeem' of monasticism and living in the wilderness of Sheheet, twenty four years wandering within the inner wilderness, five years in Pharan and five years in a cave near his home town Fisha.

Abba Bejimi the Hermit

In the Monastery of Abba Macarius the Great is a church bearing the name of "The Hermit Fathers." Within its sanctuary is an icon of Abba Bejimi, the blessed hermit father.

Our church celebrates his feast each year on the eleventh day of Kiakh. He is also mentioned in the daily 'Tasbeha'. "Pray to the Lord on our behalf my fathers...Abba Apollo, Abba Abib and Abba Bejimi; may the Lord forgive us our sins."

May their holy blessings be with us amen

28. ABBA TIMOTHY THE HERMIT

Abba Paphnatious once said: I had this desire to journey into the wilderness in order to see the saintly hermit fathers...So I walked through the wilderness for four days and nights without having anything to eat or drink. Suddenly I noticed a cave, so I approached and knocked its door (as this is a monastic habit) but no one answered. I remained at his entrance until midday, then entered his cave calling out, "Bless me father!" I saw before me a monk sitting in silence, so I stretched out my hand and held his arm. As soon as I had done this it crumbled and became as dust...I crossed myself, prayed and left.

I then walked a little further and found footprints leading to another cave. Again I knocked its door, and again no one answered. I sat at the cave's entrance and thought, 'Wherever the owner of this cave has gone, he will return, so I shall sit here and wait for him.'

I remained praying at the cave's entrance until the sun began to set, and in the distance I could see a herd of zebras with a person walking amidst them. When I approached him, I noticed that he was naked and that his hair had covered his body like a tunic. He was greatly afraid of me, and thought me to be a spirit, so abruptly he stopped and began praying. I went to him and said, "Do not be afraid father, for I am too a servant of the Lord Jesus Christ, the Son of the living God; I am not a spirit, for I have flesh and bones." He began reciting verses from the Holy Bible, then warmly greeted me. I walked him to his cave, where we prayed then sat down together. I said to him, "I greatly desired to see the hermit fathers of this wilderness, so I thank the Lord for fulfilling my desire in seeing you. My saintly father, please reveal to me your life story..."

"I was a monk residing in a monastery and enjoyed working with my hands as is the monastic habit. I used to distribute my handiwork to the weak, and the poor and the strangers. After a while, I built for myself a cell outside the monastery, and there I lived within it.

The devil, the enemy of all goodness, was never far away. He envied me for my work and so one day he came to me in the appearance of a nun who often came to buy my handiwork. Gradually, a special relationship developed between the two of us. Whenever she came to see me, we would sit together, and eat together and talk together, until one day I committed a sin with her...

For the following six months, my heart was hardened, until eventually I sat and wondered about this trial which the devil put me through, and I was deeply sorry. Realising and regretting my sin, I cried bitterly. At that moment I imagined death and the severe torment I shall face because of my sin, so I took courage and said to myself, "Arise from your sin and escape to the wilderness, and there cry with tears of repentance over your great sin and pray unceasingly to the Lord, in the hope that He will have mercy on you and forgive you!" Immediately I got up and left my solitary cell and ventured into the wilderness. Eventually the Lord lead me to this cave which is situated beside this beautiful palm tree. This tree bears twelve baskets of dates a year, and for the past thirty years, this alone has been my food. When my tunic wore out God permitted that the hair on my body grow long enough to cover me, as you can see."

I then asked this saintly hermit father, "Did you suffer at all when you first came into the wilderness to live?" He answered, "Yes I suffered greatly. Many times I threw myself to the ground because of the severity of my pain and the sorrow within my heart, and many times I felt as though I was going to die. So great was the pain that I was unable to stand for prayer, but for four years I never ceased crying and praying day and night, pleading for God to forgive me for the great sin I had committed.

It happened one day as I felt the severity of my pain worsening, that I thought to myself, 'This pain is the fruit of my impure thoughts and desires, so be patient my soul in your pain so that the Lord may heal you.' I then saw before me a man full of light saying, "Show me where your pain is?" So I pointed to my liver. He gently put his hand on the area of my pain and said to me, "You are now healed, but do not sin again. Be watchful and diligent in your prayers." And from that moment, I have lived without pain."

I Paphnatious asked if I could live with him in his cave, but he replied, "My dear brother, you could not tolerate all the Satanic wars." I then said to him, "Father, I do not yet know your name" so he answered, "My name is Timothy; please remember me in your prayers." I knelt before him and asked him to pray for me. He said, "May our beloved Lord Jesus Christ bless you and save you from all the traps of the enemy; may your ways be straight and your deeds pleasing to God, so that you may be united with your saintly fathers in the Lord's Kingdom... ." After blessing me, I returned to my cell overwhelmed with joy desiring to live the life of the hermit father Abba Timothy.

Our church celebrates his feast on the 23rd day of the blessed Coptic month Kiakh.

May his blessings be with us all, amen.

APPENDICES

QUESTIONS AND ANSWERS ABOUT THE HERMIT FATHERS

QUESTION: ARE THE HERMIT FATHERS INFALLIBLE?

Answer: No man is infallible as long as he is living on earth, only God is infallible. The life stories of the hermits tell us about the falling of some of the hermit fathers. Abba Moussa the hermit lived in ascetism for thirty years during which time even the wild beasts became friendly with him. Yet the time came when he was deceived by the devil more than once. Abba Moussa repented and the Lord sent to him Abba Samuel the Confessor, to whom he confessed to and received the sacrament of Holy Communion before passing away. Likewise Abba Timothy the hermit sinned at the beginning of his ascetic life and wept and cried for his sins until an ulcer formed in his liver. The Lord heard his prayer of repentance and sent an angel to heal him, and thus he spent the rest of his life in holiness.

QUESTION: ARE THE HERMIT FATHERS JUST SPIRITS WHO FLY FROM PLACE TO PLACE AND ENTER CHURCHES WHEN THEY ARE CLOSED WITHOUT ANYONE SEEING THEM?

Answer: The hermit fathers are humans just like us who eat, drink and sleep, but they live in complete discipline and self denial of all bodily pleasures and comfort. For example Abba Paula the First Hermit used to eat half a loaf of bread each day, delivered by a raven. Abba Noufer the hermit lived near a palm tree and used to feed from its dates, and Abba Bejimi and Abba Moussa used to eat the grass of the wilderness. All these hermits would drink from the fresh springs of mountains and rocks which God produced for them. These hermit fathers had bodies like ours that would fall sick and feel pain. As we just mentioned, Abba Timothy suffered from an ulcer in his liver, which the Lord permitted an angel to heal. At the end of Abba Noufer's life, he was struck with a terrible fever and his body turned red. Therefore, we cannot say hermits are spirits.

QUESTION: DO HERMITS WEAR CLOTHES, BECAUSE IN TIME THEIR CLOTHES WOULD WEAR OUT?

Answer: We read in the life of Abba Macarius the Great, that he saw two naked hermits wandering in the inner wilderness, just east of Libya. But this is not usual. Abba Paula the hermit clothed himself in weaved palm, Abba Noufer covered his nakedness with his long hair. One day the devil approached Abba Bejimi and persuaded him to live naked as a sign of poverty, but he wisely answered, "It is not good for me to live naked, for God provided Adam and Eve with covering for their bodies, and angels with wings to cover their feet."

From these examples we see that either God keeps their clothes from wearing out, or provides hair and animal skin/weaved palms to cover their bodies. Those who remain naked, God protects them from being seen by other humans. For example, we read in the story of St. Mary the Egyptian that she hid behind a rock when Abba Zocima approached her in the wilderness to take her blessings, and she therefore asked him to throw his garment to cover her nakedness.

QUESTION: ARE THERE A LIMITED NUMBER OF HERMITS, AND AS ONE DIES, THEY ARE REPLACED?

Answer: There is no proof to suggest that there is a limited number of hermits, as their number is unknown due to being scattered throughout the wilderness. Besides, numbering hermits indicates a community life rather than a life of solitude.

QUESTION: WHAT IS THE DIFFERENCE BETWEEN A SOLITAIRE AND A HERMIT?

Answer: A solitaire has a known cave where people may come and visit for the sake of taking their blessings. But no one knows the place of a hermit - either how to reach him, or how to return. Living in the inner wilderness, in uninhabited places, a hermit may wander for several years without seeing the face of a fellow human.

Referring to the life and progression to hermitage, Abba Issac said: "Usually a hermit begins as a monk living in a monastic community, progressing to the life of solitude (in his cell). He stays alone and keeps silent all week, only coming out of his cell on Sundays to attend the Holy Mass and meet with his fellow brothers. Then he leaves the monastic community, taking shelter as a solitaire in a cave, and lastly leaves the cave to be a lover of solitude, venturing into the inner wilderness."

CHURCHES THAT BEAR THE NAMES OF OUR HOLY HERMIT FATHERS

- Monastery of Abba Paula in the Eastern Wilderness - The church of Abba Paula the First Hermit.

- Monastery of Abba Antonious in the Eastern Wilderness - The church of Abba Antonious and Abba Paula

- Monastery of Abba Macarius in the wilderness of Sheheet - The church of The Hermit Fathers, containing the icons of Abba Samuel the Confessor, Abba Youannis the protopriest of Sheheet and friend of Abba Samuel, Abba Noufer, Abba Abram, Abba Gawargi, Abba Apollo, Abba Abib, Abba Misael and Abba Bejimi.

- Monastery of Abba Samuel the Confessor in Mount Kalamon The church of the Hermit Fathers; To the north-west of the monastery is a church bearing the name of Abba Misael the hermit. This church was consecrated by Pope Youannis, the 94th patriarch of Alexandria, on the 28th of December, 1516AD. The blessed body of Abba Bisada was placed in this church on 14 February 1977. The monastery of Abba Samuel the Confessor is one of the Fayoum monasteries. Pope Khael, the 46th patriarch of Alexandria (743-767AD), recorded that in his time there were 35 Fayoum monasteries under the care of Bishop Abram of Fayoum. Without doubt, the desert of Fayoum, including Mount Kalamon must have been home for many Holy ascetics during the fourth century.

- Monastery of Abba Balamoun the hermit , Kusr el Sayaid

- (Castle of the Hunter), Najaa Hamadi - The church of Abba Balamoun

- Monastery of St. Mary (Akhmeem) - The church of Abba Antonious and Abba Paula

- Monastery of Abba Thomas the hermit (Hajar el Sawamaa, Akhmeem)

- Monastery of the Martyrs (Akhmeem) - The church of Abba Discorus the priest, and Skapius the deacon; the two hermits and martyrs of Akhmeem

- Monastery of Abba Hermina the hermit in Kaw (Assuit)

- Monastery of Abba Hedra the hermit (Mount Aswan, west of the Nile)

- There are many churches in Upper Egypt, and Old Cairo that have altars consecrated in the names of our hermit fathers.

LITURGIES CELEBRATED IN HONOUR OF THE HERMIT FATHERS

When we read the life stories of the hermit fathers, we learn that they celebrate the Holy mass at night, especially in monasteries and old churches. Many of our church fathers and those who are pure in heart have seen these hermit fathers celebrating the liturgy.

When we read the life story of Abba Balamoun the hermit, an elder from El Kasr, Najaa Hamadi (where the monastery of Abba Balamoun is situated), tells us that when he was a young boy, he went to one of the churches in Abba Balamoun's monastery with his mother and slept the night there. His uncle was serving as a priest in the church at that time. At dawn, he sat beside his mother on the staircase, waiting for his uncle, the priest, to wake in order to begin the morning mass, when suddenly he saw a censer filled with incense moving around the church, but could not see anyone holding it. Quickly he told his mother, who took him outside to quiet him down. When the priest awoke and went into the sanctuary to begin the mass, he realised that a mass had already taken place, so in accordance with the church rites no mass can be celebrated on the same altar within nine hours, he advised the congregation that mass would be celebrated on another altar. This young boy is now serving in the monastery.

Some servants who frequently spend nights in monasteries mention that they hear soft voices singing and praying the holy mass. Many others have also recorded similar incidences, thus assuring us that hermit fathers do celebrate masses.

An archaeologist has validated the following : "There are Bedouins who move around the desert of Gabal el Nakos (Mountain of Cymbals) in the valley of El Araba, which extends from Altoor town to the monastery of Abba Antonious, the founder of monasticism and father of all monks. These Bedouins have mentioned that throughout the year they hear sounds resembling church bells." Mr. Derwish El Farr, a geologist and the manager of the Egyptian Museum of Geology states that, "the music of the sand is not imagination, but is actually heard in the valley of El Araba, as soft singing which gradually increases to become disturbing and even sometimes frightening to the listener, as there is no known source. This singing occurs on Friday and Sunday of each week." Professor Ralph Bagnold, a distinguished British scientist, who spent many years studying the Egyptian deserts, also confirms this.

Because they celebrate masses, we thus understand that some of these hermit fathers must be priests, confession fathers, and spiritual guardians. They partake in the service of the sacraments, such as the offering of the Holy Eucharist, which is the Blessed Body and Blood of our Lord Jesus Christ.

Preceding the Holy mass, the church praises some of the hermit fathers, such as in the 'tasbeha' (songs of praise): "Intercede on our behalf my two masters Abba Antonious and Abba Paula, who love their children, may He forgive us our sins...Intercede on our behalf Abba Noufer, Abba Karas and our father Paphnautios...Abba Apollo and Abba Abib and our father Abba Bejimi...all the crossbearers who perfected their faith in the wilderness..." (In the 'tasbeha' we ask for the intercession of all the saints).

In the annual Epsalmodia, is a 'doxology' for Abba Paula the First Hermit, as well as a 'doxology' for Abba Antonious and Abba Paula together. This is often sung during the consecration of a monk, or when dressing them the 'eskeem' (a belt of crosses and/or the habit of monasticism).

In the annual Epsali, is a 'doxology' which can be sung for any of the crossbearers : "...the righteous who perfected their faith, the afflicted and tormented, of whom the world does not deserve . They wander in the wilderness in caves and dens, they are ambassadors for Christ because of their faith and patience. So let us hasten along the path of their struggle towards their perfector Jesus Christ...Intercede on our behalf all the crossbearers who perfected their faith in the wilderness, that the Lord may forgive our sins..."

In the Epsaliat, are two hymns which are sung for Abba Paula the First Hermit.

In the Defnar or Memar, are the life stories and prayers for the saint of each day, and it is said before the conclusion of 'tasbeha'.

After praying the midnight psalms, the priest then asks for the intercession of all the hermit fathers, and all those who pleased the Lord : "...and the martyrs, the saints, the hermits, the ascetics and those who pleased the Lord by their good deeds from the beginning to the end of all ages, for to You is worship, the Father, Son and the Holy Spirit...Amen."

In the church Sinixarium are lives of some of the hermit fathers which are read after the Acts of the Apostles, according to their feast day.

The Commemoration in the Holy Mass : "...our righteous father Abba Antony the great, the upright Abba Paula, the three saints Macari and all their children the crossbearers. Our father Abba Noufer and our father Abba Karas, and our father Abba Paphnautios and our father Abba John the hermit, and our father Abba Bejimi...and our father Abba Misael the hermit...and the whole host of Your saints; through their prayers and supplications, have mercy upon us all and save us for the sake of Your Holy Name, that is called upon us."

The Fraction for Great Lent : "...By practicing praying and fasting, the righteous and the crossbearers escaped to the mountains, wilderness and caves, because of their tremendous love for our Lord Jesus Christ!"

The Concluding Blessing : "...through the pleadings and intercessions of...the apostles and martyrs and the righteous and all the crossbearers, the ascetics and confessors and hermits..."

WRITERS OF THE LIVES OF THE HERMIT FATHERS

We shall briefly mention the names of those who have written the life stories of some of the hermit fathers :

- Abba Paula the First Hermit –
  feast day: 2 Amshir (9 February)
  Writer: Abba Athanasius the Apostle

- Abba Noufer the hermit –
  feast day: 16 Baouna (23 June)
  Writer: Abba Paphnautios (Bebnoda)

- Abba Karas the hermit –
  feast day: 8 Abib (15 July)
  Writer: Abba Bemwakis of Sheheet

- Abba Misael the hermit -
  feast day: 13 Kiakh (22 December)
  Writer: Abba Issac, the abbot of the El Kalamon Monastery

- Abba Ghaleon the hermit –
  feast day: 13 Kiakh   (22 December)
  Writer: Abba Issac, the abbot of the El Kalamon
  Monastery

- Abba Timothy the hermit -
  feast day: 23 Kiakh   (1 January)
  Writer: Abba Paphnautios (Bebnoda)

- Abba Bejimi the hermit -
  feast day: 11 Kiakh   (20 December)
  Writer: Abba Shenouda the Archimandrite

- Abba Thomas the hermit of Mount Shenshif –
  feast day: 27 Bashans (4 June)
  Writer: Abba Wissa, Abba Shenouda's disciple

- Abba Hedra the hermit -
  feast day: 12 Kiakh   (21 December)
  Writer: Abba Bemon, his spiritual father

- Abba Balamoun the hermit -
  feast day: 25 Abib   (1 August)
  Writer: Abba Bakhomius, his disciple

- Abba Lutson the hermit –
  feast day: unknown
  Writer: Abba Isezoros the hermit, his spirirtual father

- Abba Marcos el Termaki the hermit -
  feast day: unknown
  Writer: Abba Serapion of Sheheet

- Abba Zakaria the hermit –
  feast day: unknown
  Writer: Abba Jacob the Bishop

- Abba Kyriakos the hermit –
feast day: unknown
Writer: Abba Isezoros (the deacon)

- Abba Moussa the hermit –
feast day: unknown
Writer: Abba Samuel (the priest)

- Abba Youhanna the hermit –
feast day: unknown
Writer: Abba Apollos

- Abba Issac the hermit of Mount Esna -
feast day: unknown
Writer: Abba Bacanteous

- Abba Elias the hermit of Mount Samhood –
feast day: 13 Kiakh (22 December)
Writer: unknown

- Abba Hermina the hermit –
feast day: unknown
Writer: Abba Abahor el Abarhati (el Kassar)

- St. Mary the Egyptian –
feast day: 6 Baramouda (14 April)
Writer: Abba Zocima

- Abba Simon the Stylite –
feast day: unknown
Writer: Abba Bemwa, priest of Sheheet

- Abba Bamoun the Stylite –
feast day: unknown
Writer: Abba Bemwa, priest of Sheheet

- Abba Discorus and Skapius his brother of Mount Akhmeem –
feast day: 1 Tuba (9 January)
Writer: unknown

- Abba Alian the hermit of the Eastern Mountain –
feast day: unknown
Writer: Abba Khristozolos the hermit

- Abba Stephanos the hermit –
feast day: unknown
Writer: unknown

- St. Annasimon the hermit and queen -
feast day: unknown
Writer: unknown

- Abba Daniel the protopriest of Sheheet -
feast day: unknown
Writer: unknown

- Abba Yousab the hermit –
feast day: unknown
Writer: unknown

- Abba Silasi the hermit –
feast day: unknown
Writer: unknown

- Abba Ezekial the hermit –
feast day: unknown
Writer: unknown

- Abba Mar Olag el Sabaii the hermit –
feast day: 10 Abib (17 July)
Writer: Abba Mar Okeen, his disciple

Many stories of the hermit fathers have also been written by Abba Issac, the abbot of the Kalamon Monastery, Abba Macarius the writer, Abba Boctor the writer, Abba Macarius the Great, Abba Paphnautios and several others.

Abba Palladius who wrote the life stories of our fathers the monks, tells us about Dioklees the hermit who dwelt on Mount Ansana: "He was an expert in many languages and in the science of philosophy. When he was twenty eight years old, he heard God's call and so left everything to be alone with Christ. He lived in a cave for thirty five years. He believed that, 'once the mind is not consumed with spiritual contemplations, it becomes easy to fall victim to bodily desires.' Dortheous the priest lived in a nearby cave and served the hermits who lived in the surrounding region...he also lived during the time of St. Milania the Younger."

This is just a small number of the numerous hermit fathers who have blessed our church throughout the ages. We have numerous martyrs, confessors, hermits, archimandrites, ascetics and cross-bearers, however, history has not been fortunate enough to record all the life stories of our hermit fathers...those who lived in the faith of God...

And now, for the Glory of His name, we shall begin recalling the life stories of some of the hermit fathers, whose stories have not been printed before...

GLOSSARY OF TERMS

ABBA - Coptic word meaning 'father', or within a monastic community it is given to the spiritual father/elder. It is also a title given to the Pope and to bishops, and also to some of our fathers the saints.

AGAPE - The primary meaning is 'love'. It is also used to mean the meal taken in common after the celebration of the Liturgy.

ARCHIMANDRITE - A title given to the abbot/protopriest of a monastery.

BEDOUIN - An Arab of the desert; a nomad, a wanderer.

CELL - A hut or cave where the monk lives alone or with a disciple. These buildings are scattered about the desert, and a group of such cells is called a lavra.

COENOBITIC MONASTICISM - A type of monasticism established by Abba Bakhomious, Father of the Community, in the third century, where monks or nuns live a communal life in a monastery or convent.

CROSSBEARER - A title given to hermits who struggled relentlessly in the life of monasticism. They are considered crossbearers because the strife they endured can be compared to the suffering involved in bearing the cross. This title has also been given to some of the Confessors and martyrs.

DEFNAR - A collection of short stories of the saints of each day, and it is read in the monasteries during the Midnight Praise.

DOXOLOGY - Songs of praises for saints and for special occasions.

EPSAL/EPSALIA - Songs of praise for our Lord Jesus Christ.

EPSALMODIA - Book containing midnight psalms and praises.

ESKEEM - A leather belt of crosses which is worn by a monk who has reached a very high level of spirituality. This belt symbolises spiritual responsibility and struggle, as well as self control over bodily needs and desires. The 'eskeem' may also be the monastic habit.

FARAGIA - A black tunic worn by monks and priests. It is black because it symbolizes the fact that they have died completely to the world, and everything in the world, and are now devoting their life to Christ.

HERMITS - Better known as Anchorites, the Spirit Born. They are usually called "El Souah" in Arabic. This type of monk has reached a very high level of spirituality where his spirit is heavier than his body, because he is fervent in spirit, and he rarely eats. They live in groups and can easily move from one place to another in a very short time, without anyone seeing them.

HESSIAN - A strong, coarse fabric woven from plant fibres. It is commonly used for sacks and carpet backing.

HERSYCHIA - A Greek word meaning stillness, quiet, tranquillity. This is the central consideration in the prayer of the Desert Fathers. On the external level, it signifies an individual living as a solitary; on a deeper level, it is the possession of interior quiet and peace. More specifically it means guarding the mind, constant remembrance of God, and the possession of inner prayer.

KOLONSOWA - A hood usually embroided with crosses, that is worn on the head by all monks. It is believed that the angel of the Lord had passed on the 'kolonsowa' and monastic habit to St. Anthony, father of monasticism, and to this day, it is worn by all Coptic and Syrian monks. Catholic Franschescan monks and other Orthodox monks also wear a 'kolonsowa', but usually with no embrodied crosses.

HOLY THURSDAY - The Thursday before Good Friday, commemorating the Lord's Last Supper. It is better known as Maundy Thursday.

METANYIA - Prostration. There are three different reasons why we prostrate:-

- for worship; when we enter the church and prostrate before the Holy Altar

- for respect; in the presence of a Pope or bishop, we prostrate before them.

- Repentance, interior sorrow for sin. It also means the action by which such sorrow is expressed, usually a prostration, or 'metanyia'.

MELOTE - Sheepskin. A monastic cloak made of sheepskin, also used as a blanket for the monk to sleep on.

MEMAR - Remembrance of the saints.

SHEIK EL ROHANI - Literally, it is the Arabic term for 'Spiritual Elder', however, this title has been given specifically to the saintly father Abba Youhanna Saba.

SINIXARIUM - A collection of detailed biographies of the saints of each day, and their stories are read during the Holy Mass (after the Acts of the Apostles).

STYLITE - Men who have lived for very long periods on the top of a pillar.

TASBEHA - Collection of Doxologies and praises.

TONYA - A white tunic worn by all monks and priests while celebrating the Holy Mass. It is white because it represents the joyous angels who are serving God in purity and holiness.

REFERENCES

1. The Holy Liturgy Book
2. The Book of Praise - 'Epsalmodia'
3. The Coptic Church Sinixarium
4. The Precious Stories of Saints - Maximos Mazloom
5. The Paradise of the Fathers
6. Guide to the Coptic Museum - Marcos Semeka
7. History of our Precious Church - H.G. Bishop Isizoros
8. Monks and Monasteries - Very Reverend Father Abdelmessieh El Masoudy
9. History of the Coptic Nation - Father Manassa Youhanna
10. Christianity - H.G. Bishop Dioskoros
11. Release of the Spirit - H.H. Pope Shenouda III
12. The Spirituality of Praise, 'Tasbeha' - H.G. Bishop Mettaos
13. Abba Balamoun the Hermit - St. George Bookshop in Shikolany
14. Abba Hermina the Hermit of Mount Kaw - Nabil Saleem
15. The Martyrs Abba Bakhoum and his sister Dalosham – Nabil Saleem
16. Abba Latson the Hermit - Amir Nasr
17. Abba John the Short - Very Reverend Father Misael Bahr
18. St. Mary the Egyptian and Abba Zocima - El Mahaba Bookshop
19. Abba Bijimi, a Monk from the El Sourian Monastery
20. The Upright Abba Paula - Yousef Habib
21. The Sayings of the Desert Fathers - Benedicta Ward SLG
22. The Arabic 'El Keraza' (1965, 1975, 1977, 1978)
23. Monks of the Coptic Monasteries (Video) - Victor Messieh, Sydney 1992

FURTHER READING

- Bell, David N., *The Life of Shenoute by Besa*, Kalamazoo 1983
- Budge E. A. Wallis, *The Paradise of the Holy Fathers*, 2 Volumes, Texas 1994.
- Burton-Christie, Douglas, *The Word in the Desert. Scripture and the Quest for Holiness in Early Christian Monasticism*, New York and Oxford 1993.
- Brock Sebastian, *The Syriac Fathers on Prayer and the Spiritual Life*, Kalamazoo.
- Chitty, Derwas, *The Desert a City*, Oxford 1966.
- Chryssavgis John, *Abba Isaiah of Scetis, Ascetic Discourses*. Kalamazoo 2002.
- Climacus John, *The Ladder Of Divine Ascent*, Boston Massachusetts 1991.
- Harmless, William, *Desert Christians: an introduction to the literature of early monasticism*, New York 2004.
- Meyer, Robert T., *Palladius: The Lausiac History*. Ancient Christian Writers 34, New York 1965.
- Russell, Norman, *The Lives of the Desert Fathers. The Historia Monachorum in Aegypto*, Kalamazoo 1981
- St Augustine, *Confessions of St Augustine*. 1961
- St Isaac of Nineveh, *St Isaac of Nineveh, On Ascetical Life*. New York 1998.
- Stewart, Columba, *The World of the Desert Fathers: Stories and Sayings from the Anonymous Series of the "Apophthegmata Patrum"*, Oxford 1986.
- *The Philokalia, The Complete Text 4 Volumes*, London 1979.
- Veilleux, Armand, *Pachomian Koinonia*. 3 vols., Cistercian Studies Series 45-47. Kalamazoo 1981-1982.
- Vivian, Tim, *Four Desert Fathers. Pambo, Evagrius, Macarius of Egypt & Macarius of Alexandria*. Popular Patristics Series, New York 2004.

- Vivian, Tim, *Journeying into God. Seven Early Monastic Lives*, Minneapolis 1996

- Vivian, Tim, *St Macarius the Spiritbearer. Coptic Texts Relating to Saint Macarius the Great.* Popular Patristic Series, New York 2004.

- Vivian, Tim, and Apostolos Athanassakis, *Athanasius of Alexandria, The Life of Antony. The Coptic Life and the Greek Life.* Cistercian Studies Series 202, Kalamazoo 2003.

- Ward, Benedicta, *The Sayings of the Desert Fathers: The Alphabetical Collection*, Cistercian Studies 59, Kalamazoo 1984.

- Ward, Benedicta, *The Wisdom of the Desert Fathers: The "Apophthegmata Patrum" (from the Anonymous Series)*, Oxford 1986.

ALSO PUBLISHED BY
ST SHENOUDA MONASTERY

Title: The Life of St Shenouda the Archimandrite and some of His Sayings.
Translated by: Fiby Henein
Edited by: The Monks of the Monastery
Year: First Edition 2004

The Coptic tradition venerates St Shenouda as a hero of monasticism. During his life thousands of monks and nuns in his monastery in Akhmim looked to him as their *abba*, the father of their spiritual and material lives. Today, 1600 years later his life is venerated in his monasteries in Akhmim and in Sydney, Australia, hundreds of miles away from his home town.

This book gives a quick sketch of the saint's life translated from Arabic, as well as a pictorial tour through the monasteries of the saint, in Akhmim and Sydney.

Title: The Life of Saint Wissa
(the Disciple of Saint Shenouda)
and Selected Sayings
Edited by: The Monks of the Monastery
Year: First Edition 2004

Saint Wisa is among the group of saints that are called 'Disciples' in the monastic life, e.g. Theodore the disciple of Saint Pachomios, and Ezekiel the disciple of Saint Paul of Tamouh. These saints were called 'Disciples' because they lived in honesty, and loyal to their leaders. They learnt from them in total obedience, adopting their virtues.

This book highlights the little we know about the saint's life, it also offers an English translation of some of his writings.

Title: The Sublime Life of Monasticism
Author: H.G. Bishop Mettaous
Translated by: One of the Blessed Ladies
Edited by: The Monks of the Monastery
Year: First Edition 2005

Many books were published recently about the lives of the desert monks which drew many youth to the monastic life, but they usually leave one question unanswered "What are the signs of the monastic calling?"

This book contains many spiritual experiences of a monk who has tasted the sweetness of this life in the wilderness of Scetis and I hope that through this book you will find the answer to this question. We pray that God may bless the monastic life in our church through the prayers of H.H. Pope Shenouda III, the father of all monks of our days, who encourages monasticism and returned it to its glorious days.

Title: Pimonakhos *(The Monk)*
Edited by: The Monks of the Monastery
Email: pimonakhos@copticmail.com

A monthly newsletter with monastic issues for today's youth. The newsletter deals with issues scarcely talked about today such as Celibacy, Obedience, and Voluntary poverty.

Each issue is usually made up of an article by the Pope or one of the Bishops, an excerpt from a book, and an article by one of the youth. Every issue has two books suggested for further reading on different monastic issues.

To receive this newsletter monthly by email, send your request to the email above.

Lightning Source UK Ltd.
Milton Keynes UK

176576UK00005B/1/P